Diego Hurtado de Mendoza

Twayne's World Authors Series
Spanish Literature

Janet Perez, Editor
Texas Tech University

TWAS 794

DIEGO HURTADO DE MENDOZA
*Photograph reproduced by permission of the
Galleria Palatina, Pitti Palace, Florence.*

Diego Hurtado de Mendoza

By David H. Darst

Florida State University

Twayne Publishers
A Division of G.K. Hall & Co. • Boston

Diego Hurtado de Mendoza

David H. Darst

Copyright 1987 by G.K. Hall & Co.
All rights reserved.
Published by Twayne Publishers
A Division of G.K. Hall & Co.
70 Lincoln Street
Boston, Massachusetts 02111

Copyediting supervised by Lewis DeSimone
Book production by Janet Zietowski
Book design by Barbara Anderson

Typeset in 11 pt. Garamond
by P&M Typesetting, Inc. Waterbury, Connecticut

Printed on permanent/durable acid-free paper
and bound in the United States of America

Library of Congress Cataloging in Publication Data

Darst, David H.
  Diego Hurtado de Mendoza.

  (Twayne's world authors series ; TWAS 794. Spanish literature)
  Bibliography: p.
  Includes index.
  1. Hurtado de Mendoza, Diego, 1503–1575—Criticism
and interpretation. I. Title. II. Series: Twayne's
world authors series ; TWAS 794. III. Series: Twayne's
world authors series. Spanish literature.
PQ6399.Z5D37   1987   861'.3   87-11932
ISBN 0-8057-6648-0

For Carmen

Contents

About the Author

David H. Darst received his collegiate degrees from the University of the South (Sewanee), the University of North Carolina at Chapel Hill, and the University of Kentucky, respectively. Since 1970 he has taught in the Department of Modern Languages and the Program in the Humanities at Florida State University. His professional credentials include a Fulbright Fellowship to Spain, research grants from the National Endowment for the Humanities and the American Philosophical Society, a score of articles on all aspects of Spanish civilization of the Golden Age, and four books: *The Comic Art of Tirso de Molina* (1974), *Tirso de Molina's the Trickster of Seville: A Critical Commentary* (1976), *Juan Boscán* (1978), and *Imitatio: Polémicas sobre la imitación en el siglo de oro* (1985).

Preface

Diego Hurtado de Mendoza is one of the most renowned Spanish writers of the first half of the sixteenth century, and more is known concerning his life and times than about any other poet of the period. In the 1850s Adolfo de Castro republished for the first time Diego Hurtado de Mendoza's poetic works in the *Poetas líricos de los siglos XVI y XVII* volume of *Biblioteca de Autores Españoles* (32:52–103), and Cayetano Rosell did an edition of the *Guerra de Granada* for the *Historiadores de sucesos particulares* volume of the same series (21:65–122). Two Frenchmen, R. Foulché-Delbosc and A. Morel-Fatio, then edited a number of his letters and minor literary pieces. During the same time, William I. Knapp complemented his earlier work on Juan Boscán with a five-hundred-page edition of don Diego's *Obras poéticas: primera edición completa* for volume II of *Colección de Libros Españoles Raros o Curiosos*.

One would think that these scholarly productions would assure Diego Hurtado de Mendoza's continued prestige; yet little substantial material was produced on him for the next seventy years except for the studies of Foulché-Delbosc and Morel-Fatio in France, two minor pieces of literary history by J. P. W. Crawford in the United States, and a valuable collection of letters compiled by Alberto Vázquez and R. Selden Rose, published at Yale in 1935 with the title *Algunas cartas de don Diego Hurtado de Mendoza escritas 1538–1552*. Nevertheless, after the Spanish Civil War don Diego was blessed with a definitive edition of his *Guerra de Granada* by Manuel Gómez-Moreno in the Royal Academy's *Memorial Histórico Español* (vol. 49), and with a definitive survey of his life and works by Angel González Palencia and Eugenio Mele, appropriately entitled *Vida y obras de don Diego Hurtado de Mendoza*. Finally, in the 1960s, the American historian Erika Spivakovsky became interested in the Spanish diplomat and published a series of articles on his political career, culminating in her authoritative *Son of the Alhambra*. Spivakovsky's work alone established don Diego as the single nonroyal person in sixteenth-century Spain about whom the most is known, and it clearly made his life and times the most accessible to those who are not thoroughly familiar with the Spanish language.

The present Twayne book complements and supplements the work of these preceding scholars. Chapter 1 on the life and times of Diego Hurtado de Mendoza logically borrows much from Spivakovsky, and from González Palencia and Mele, by condensing and better organizing their information. Chapter 3 on the *Guerra de Granada* draws much of its information from earlier editions, and in particular from the most recent text by Bernardo Blanco-González for Editorial Castalia in 1970. Chapter 2 on the poetry is justifiably the longest and most complete part of the book, for it is precisely Diego Hurtado de Mendoza's poetry that has been the most neglected of his writings. Chapter 4 examines some of the works that over the years have been attributed to Diego Hurtado de Mendoza, especially the *Lazarillo de Tormes,* whose literary qualities have been examined by Peter N. Dunn in *The Spanish Picaresque Novel* and by Robert L. Fiore in *Lazarillo de Tormes.*

The format and style of this book follow the general pattern of all studies in Twayne's World Authors Series. Translations have been provided for most of the Spanish quotations. The text utilized when citing from Diego Hurtado de Mendoza's writings as well as from historians and critics is, in every case but one, the most accessible printing or edition. The exception is William I. Knapp's *Obras poéticas de D. Diego Hurtado de Mendoza,* which remains the most complete compilation of the Spaniard's poetry. Knapp's edition was done in 1877, when accentuation, capitalization, and punctuation were different from today's style; so for the convenience of the reader those grammatical peculiarities have been modernized. This volume also follows standard practice by anglicizing the names of internationally known figures (such as Charles V, Philip II, Paul III), but retaining the vernacular forms for lesser known personages as well as for those Spaniards better recognized by their native names, as are Juana, Isabel, don Juan de Austria, and others. Finally, there is the problem of the subject's name. Today he is known as Diego Hurtado de Mendoza, so libraries and bibliographies list him under Hurtado. In the sixteenth and seventeenth centuries, however, he was known simply as Diego de Mendoza; and, since all critics and historians to the present have continued to refer to him simply as Mendoza, he will be so styled in this Twayne volume.

David H. Darst

Florida State University

Chronology

Chapter One
The Life and Times of Diego Hurtado de Mendoza
Childhood and Education

If ever a poet came into the world with a silver spoon in his mouth, it was Diego Hurtado de Mendoza. He was born in 1504 in the Alhambra of Granada.[1] His father was Iñigo López de Mendoza, second count of Tendilla, who had been occupying the palatial Alhambra since 1492, when the Catholic monarchs Ferdinand and Isabel named him the first captain-general of the newly acquired kingdom of Granada. The Moorish king Boabdil had abandoned the Alhambra on 2 January, when he and the Moorish residents surrendered the city to the Christians, and Ferdinand and Isabel had given it to Tendilla as payment for his services during the campaign to take the city.

The Mendoza family was therefore not from Granada, nor were they even from the surrounding area. They were from a long line of "cristianos viejos" (Old Christians) from the North, and their ancestry could be traced directly to the time of Spain's national hero the Cid, when Lope López de Mendoza was majordomo to doña Urraca, Queen of Castile. By the 1300s, the family had prospered enough to establish a permanent family residence in Guadalajara in the grand style of the medieval Castilian palace.

The first known poet in the family was another, earlier Diego Hurtado de Mendoza (1365–1404), the great-great-grandfather of the author of *Guerra de Granada;* but he was overshadowed literarily by his famous son Iñigo López de Mendoza, the Marqués de Santillana (1398–1458), the most prestigious poet of the Spanish fifteenth century.[2]

The Marqués de Santillana had seven sons. The oldest, named Diego Hurtado de Mendoza, as was his grandfather, became the second Marqués de Santillana. The fifth born, Pedro González de Mendoza (1428–95), eventually became the grand cardinal of Spain; he is today known to millions because a very fine Spanish cognac, "Cardinal Mendoza," bears his name. Don Diego's grandfather was the *seg-undón* of the family, Iñigo López de Mendoza, the first count of Tendilla. Unfortunately, the count and his family sided with Juana "la Beltraneja" in the dispute over who should inherit the Castilian crown after Henry IV "el Impotente" (d. 1474). King Henry was reportedly impotent, hence his epithet, and his half-sister Isabel claimed that she should rightfully inherit the throne of Castile. Juana, the first-born daughter by Henry's second marriage, was considered illegitimately sired by the duke of Albuquerque Beltrán de la Cueva, who was a nephew by marriage of don Diego's grandfather. It was therefore clear that the powerful Mendoza clan would support their "relative" if the question of accession to the throne should lead to a civil war. That outcome was inevitable when Isabel secretly married Ferdinand of Aragón in 1469 and Juana la Beltraneja was betrothed to the Portuguese king Alfonso V, establishing thereby a clear east-west demarcation for the ensuing struggle for the crown.[3]

The distinguished career of the Mendoza family could have easily come to a jolting halt at that point in history if Ferdinand and Isabel had not gone out of their way to entice them over to the Castilian-Aragonese alliance. Along with the normal titles, lands, and marriage alliances bestowed on the Mendoza family in the years between 1469 and 1474, Ferdinand named don Pedro to the cardinalate in 1473, thus binding him and the family to the Isabeline side. Regrettably for the posterity of the family name, it was this same Cardinal Mendoza who in 1482 became archbishop of Toledo and then insisted that Ferdinand establish the Inquisition in Spain, with the infamous Tomás de Torquemada as the first grand inquisitor.

Iñigo López de Mendoza (1420–79), don Diego's grandfather, was made count of Tendilla in 1465 by Henry IV. Of all the sons of the Marqués de Santillana, he was the most adept in military matters. His son, also Iñigo López de Mendoza (1442–1515), the second count of Tendilla (and from 1512 the first Marqués de Mondejar), followed the military career of his father; but he was also one of the first to introduce Italian humanism into Spain. Although he spent most of his adult life either fighting the Moors around Granada or ruling them, he went to Italy for two years in 1485 as envoy to Pope Innocent VIII and returned with Italian architects (who built the Colegio de Santa Cruz in Valladolid), a hoard of books, and, of most importance, the young teacher Pietro Martire d'Anghiera, who would be the resident humanist at the court of Ferdinand and Isabel.[4]

By 1492, don Iñigo had become the commanding general of the Spanish forces in the South, so his appointment as captain-general of Granada was a logical one, and a position that don Iñigo not only retained for the next twenty-three years of his life but which he turned into a hereditary post by passing it on to his son and grandson. In 1480, he had married doña Francisca Pacheco, one of the children of Juan Pacheco (1419–74), Marqués de Villena and Maestre de Santiago, the man who virtually ran Castile during the last years of the reign of Henry IV. Pacheco was therefore a supporter of Juana la Beltraneja, as was his son, the second Marqués de Villena; yet after the civil war the Pachecos were pardoned by Queen Isabel and granted positions within the Castilian government.

When doña Francisca and her husband settled into the Alhambra, she had already borne at least three children: María (ca. 1482–?), Antonio Hurtado (1489–1566), and Antonio (1491–1552). She eventually gave don Iñigo five more: María Pacheco (d. 1531), Bernardino (d. 1557), Francisco (d. 1544), Isabel (–?), and, the youngest, Diego Hurtado. The parents and children lived in the Alhambra with the same luxury as did the earlier Arab residents. A German visitor to the Alhambra in 1495 described his visit in the following words:

Finally we entered the Alhambra. Passing through many iron doors and through various rooms of soldiers and officials, we came to the sumptuous and noble palace of the Mayor don Iñigo López, count of Tendilla, of the Castilian house of Mendoza, who having read the letter that the mayor of Almería gave us for him, received us with many gestures of love and friendship. He spoke to me in Latin, because he is very learned; and, understanding him perfectly, I answered in the same language. He had us sit on silk rugs; he ordered cold refreshments brought; and then, followed by a splendid squad of soldiers, he accompanied us in person to visit the royal palace, in which we saw rooms with pavements of the whitest marble, delightful gardens with lemon trees, myrtles, pools with marble sides, four rooms full of weapons, like lances, crossbows, swords, cuirasses, and arrows; bedrooms and dressing rooms; marble fountains with water spouts in many salons larger than those in Saint Augustine; a bathing room marvellously vaulted and, next to it, a bedroom; very high columns, a patio that has in its center a large marble fountain sustained by twelve lions of the same stone that spout water from their mouths as from reeds; many flagstones fifteen feet long and seven or eight feet wide, and others ten and eleven feet square. . . . In summary, I don't think that in Europe anything similar can be found, since it is all so magnificent, so majestic, so exquisitely worked, that neither he who contemplates it can convince himself that he isn't in a paradise, nor would it be possible for me to make an exact report of all I saw. The count accompanied us constantly, giving us full explanations about each thing.[5]

By 1508, the family had become so attached to Andalucía that don Diego's father told a Castilian friend he considered himself a "native" Granadan and did not plan to leave the kingdom ever again.[6] By all accounts, Tendilla was liked by the Moors he ruled and always took their side against the religious and political reactionaries when feasible. He was, in short, the "king" of Granada for the new Spaniards he controlled. Don Diego describes the politics during the early years of Granada in his *Guerra de Granada*, and that subject will be treated at length in chapter 3. It is sufficient here to note that by the time don Diego was born in 1504, the Mendoza family was well adjusted to the customs and ways of their Arab residents. The opposite was not the case, however. The Moors had rebelled against their Christian overlords in 1500 and had had to be subdued by a large army under King Ferdinand and Gonzálo Fernández de Córdoba.[7] The consequences were disastrous for the Moors, for they legally ceased to exist as such, becoming, as of 2 February 1502, *moriscos,* that is, "new Christians"; for conversion or deportation was now demanded of all unbaptized Arabs in Spain. The writer don Diego thus never knew any *moros,* for by the time he was born all had been forcibly converted to the true faith. He also probably did not know his mother, who died sometime before 1508. His father never remarried, so the child was more than likely raised by Morisco servants. It was inevitable that he would become fluent in Arabic at a young age, since that was the native language of Granada, and in the *Guerra de Granada* Mendoza shows a command of Arabic terminology; but as far as can be determined he never used his knowledge of the language for artistic or literary purposes.

There is no reason to suppose that the young Diego's views on religion were significantly altered by his constant exposure to people who were Christians in name only. It is indeed true that not one of don Diego's artistic writings is religious in nature, nor do his letters reflect any Catholic fervor; and his *Guerra de Granada* actually downplays religious motives for the rebellion, stressing political and economic abuses. Erika Spivakovsky can thus claim that "Catholic orthodoxies did not hold don Diego in thrall; he showed little need for religion—an atypical trait in a Spaniard" (Spivakovsky, 24). She gives the Arab environment in which don Diego was raised as the major reason for his disinterest in religion; but that kind of argument does not jibe with trends in the Renaissance. Juan Boscán and Garcilaso de la Vega were not brought up in Moorish households, and the writings of neither show any more religious inclinations than do those of Mendoza. The same is true for the Italian contemporaries Niccolo Machiavelli and Baldassare Castiglione. Were they also raised among new Christians? Diego Hurtado de Mendoza was a product and reflection of his age—the first half of the sixteenth century—an age in which artistic and humanistic interests were either consciously divorced from religion (if the person were secure in his cultural milieu and wrote principally as an intellectual exercise) or were consciously incorporated into religion (if the person were relatively insecure in his cultural milieu and wrote principally as part of his profession). Mendoza, Boscán, Garcilaso, Cetina, and in general the entire school of Castilian poets at the court of Charles V belong to the former group.

It is not known when don Diego joined the cadre of courtiers who traveled throughout Europe in the emperor's service, nor is much known about the youth's education and early trips from Granada. Charles was in Granada during the summer and fall of 1526, and don Diego, then twenty-two years old, would have certainly participated in the festivities that were held to celebrate Charles's recent marriage to Isabel, the daughter of King John of Portugal. This would also be the latest date at which don Diego would have met Francisco de los Cobos (ca. 1477–1547), at that time one of Charles's many secretaries, who was to be eventually the emperor's closest advisor and Mendoza's most trusted friend.[8] Almost everything that is known about the private life of Mendoza comes from the letters he wrote to Francisco de los Cobos from Venice in the 1540s (Vázquez and Rose, 9–111).

There is in fact only one document that refers to the formative years of don Diego, and it is not very precise. In 1575, Ambrosio de Morales published his book *Las antigüedades de las ciudades de España* with a dedication to Diego Hurtado de Mendoza which, according to Morales, was based on information supplied by Mendoza himself:

Having studied Latin, Greek, and Arabic in Granada and Salamanca, and afterwards Civil and Canon Law; and having traveled through a good part of Spain to see and excavate faithfully its ancient stones, you went to Italy where, following the war at the rank your person merited, you divided your time by spending the summers in the war and the winters going to Rome and Padua and other universities where there were famous teachers like Augustine Nypho, Montes de Oca, and others to learn from them logic, philosophy, and mathematics.[9]

Another fact relating to Mendoza's whereabouts during the early period is a reference in the *Historia de la vida y hechos del emperador Carlos V* by Fray Prudencio de Sandoval that mentions "Don Diego de Mendoza" as the commander of a company of troops at the Battle of Pavia in 1525.[10] If the reference alludes to Diego Hurtado de Mendoza, then he entered the circle of courtiers accompanying Charles V quite early, and probably returned to Spain with Charles to attend the meeting of the Cortes in Toledo that fall. Don Diego also reveals in a letter that he went to Portugal once with his sister, who died in 1531 (González Palencia and Mele, 1:61–62). The most likely time for him to have done this would be in the spring of 1526 when an entourage of Spanish nobles went to Portugal to accompany Isabel, the daughter of the Portuguese king, to Granada, where she married Charles V. And it is known that Mendoza did attend the Cortes in Toledo, because he makes two references in letters to the Duque de Alba concerning their youthful exploits in the imperial city.[11] According to Spivakovsky (36), Alba and Mendoza could have been in Toledo at the same time only during the Cortes of 1525. This point will be of major importance when the authorship of *Lazarillo de Tormes* is examined in chapter 4.

There is also some justification for believing that don Diego may have studied in Siena for the next two years. González Palencia and Mele (1:65–69) cite three Sienese chroniclers—Alessandro Sozzini, Angiolo Bardi, and Antonio Pecci—who report that Mendoza stayed in Siena for two years. If Mendoza was in Siena, it would have to have been between 1527 and 1529; but the whole matter may be fictional, since no substantial records for the sojourn exist.

In summary, there is not much solid information on Mendoza's first twenty-five years. Most of the leads to his whereabouts and doings are either secondhand or recollective, and none give specific dates of time periods. Fortunately, don Diego's next twenty-five years can be charted with supreme accuracy because of the enormous store of records and letters that he kept and wrote.

Mendoza's Years with the Emperor

Mendoza's diplomatic career evidently began in 1529, the first year in which his name appears in the records as a member of the emperor's staff. Charles had left Barcelona in July 1529 to meet Pope Clement VII in Bologna, where the Spanish King Charles I would be crowned the Holy Roman Emperor Charles V. The trip through Genoa, Piacenza, Parma, and Reggio took four months, and Charles then waited three more months in Bologna until his coronation 24 February. It is known from a number of Italian chronicles that "don Diego di Mendoza" was present at the festivities in Bologna (Spivakovsky, 47). After the coronation, don Diego must have returned to Granada, because he settled some legal matters there with his brother in 1531 (Gonzáles Palencia and Mele, 1:58).

Mendoza's name next appears among those who participated in the capture of La Goleta and Tunis from Barbarossa in 1535. There are no records of his whereabuts between 1531 and 1535. He could very well have been with the emperor, who returned to Spain via Barcelona in 1533 and held Cortes in Madrid during December 1534. The siege of Tunis was one of those engagements more reminiscent of the late Middle Ages than of the Renaissance. By all accounts, just about every Spaniard with noble blood took part in it, including don Diego's two brothers Francisco and Bernardino, the last of whom was made governor of La Goleta when Charles returned to the Continent in August. What don Diego's official duties were during the siege—if he had any—is unknown. This is nonetheless an important matter, because there exists an anonymous tract entitled "Lo de La Goleta y Túnéz, año de 1535" that could very well be by Mendoza. The text will be discussed in chapter 4.

Although Barbarossa slipped through the emperor's blockade and continued to harrass the Spanish seaboard for years to come, the campaign is rightly considered by most historians as the culmination of Spain's military hegemony. In the words of R. Trevor Davies, "the taking of Tunis is the high-water mark of Spanish power in northern Africa as it is the high-water mark of Charles's reputation in Europe."[12] Don Diego rightly remembers it with pride as late as 1567 in a letter to Philip II (Spivakovsky, 53–54); and he at least had gained something from the sack of the city that followed its surrender, for he mentions in *Guerra de Granada* that he brought out of Africa a number of Arabic books which he reread in preparation for the section on Granada in his chronicle.[13]

From Tunis, Charles—and presumably don Diego—sailed to Sicily and then up the coast to Naples, where the emperor spent the entire winter from November to late March. From there the imperial entourage moved to Rome for a series of important conferences in April with Pope Paul III. Charles needed the pope's allegiance in the religious matter of subduing the German Protestants and in the secular matter of halting the advances of Francis I in Italy. The pope refused to take sides, and Charles stormed out of Rome to engage the French army. As usual, however, events in the imperial realm transpired at truly a snail's pace. It took Charles a full three months to move from Rome to Savigliano; and he did not engage the French until August. The invasion of Provence gained nothing, and Charles was back in Italy within a month and in Spain by December. The only memorable event in the campaign was the loss of the poet Garcilaso de la Vega. Mendoza had a military role in the expedition, according to one report,[14] and more than likely he was at Garcilaso's side when he died.

It is at this time that Mendoza received his first international mission. While in Rome, Charles learned of the death of his aunt Catherine of Aragon, the first wife of Henry VIII who was divorced by him so he could marry Ann Boleyn. The emperor had broken relations with Henry over the divorce, but now that Catherine and Ann Boleyn (beheaded by Henry the same year) were both dead and Henry was "legally" married to Jane Seymour, Charles saw an opportunity to renew political alliances with the English and thus encircle France. He therefore sent a new ambassador to England to discuss the possible marriage of Henry's daughter Mary with Charles's brother-in-law Luis of Portugal, and the new envoy was none other than Diego Hurtado de Mendoza.

There are fortunately a number of records of don Diego's visit to England from May 1537 to September 1538, when he left to become ambassador to the Republic of Venice. From the details of his visit,[15] it is known that he frequented the court of Henry VIII, that he traveled around the country, and that he detested everything about England. In a letter to Francisco de los Cobos on 20 February 1538, Mendoza complained at length about the weather, having nothing to do, and the plague bells: "I'm well, and although there have been no frosts in this country, I am as frozen as if I were in Russia; the health of this place is no better. As a man frightened by each tolling of the bell, I take your counsel and flee fifteen miles. . . . And although it is a good life here for those accustomed to it, I would prefer Barcelona" (Vázquez and Rose, 3). To frustrate him even more, during 1537–38 Charles had made a complete about-face in diplomatic alliances. In November 1537, the emperor signed a truce with France; and in June 1538, he, Francis I, and Pope Paul III met in Nice and formed a ten-year alliance. Charles then traveled with Pope Paul to Genoa and arranged for a Holy League against the Ottoman Turks which would ally the two of them to the Doge of Venice. Henry VIII was rightly disturbed by this grand alliance of the continental powers and began to treat don Diego rather coldly during the spring and summer of 1538. Don Diego was recalled in August—since there really was nothing more for a Spanish ambassador to do in England—and returned to Toledo via Brussels, Breda, and France (demonstrating thereby the new security created by the Franco-Spanish treaty). He was in Toledo before Christmas, 1538, when Charles was holding another Cortes, and shortly thereafter embarked to take over his new ambassadorship to the Republic of Venice, where he arrived on 25 July 1539.

Mendoza's Italian Sojourn

Diego Hurtado de Mendoza's arrival in Venice could not have been at a worse time. A drought had devastated the northeast of Italy and the peasants were pouring into the cities in search of food and work. Mendoza took up residence in a palace on the Grand Canal and immediately began intriguing in both foreign and domestic matters. The first item on his list of duties was evidently to make a quick profit from the drought and starvation. His letters to Francisco de los Cobos—to whom he now writes at least once a month—trace his efforts to manipulate the wheat market in Italy. In November he explained to Cobos a grand plan to buy a shipment of wheat in Naples from the viceroy to sell in Venice at an enormous profit ("de manera que quedo rico," "so I'll be wealthy" [Vázquez and Rose, 19]). In December he brought Cobos up to date on the venture, complaining that the viceroy would only sell him half the wheat he needed, and urging Cobos to use his political influence in Naples to push the deal through. Finally, in May 1540 Mendoza reported the viceroy permitted him to buy all the grain, but he added that the grain came so late he made very little profit.

Other matters that fill Mendoza's letters are, first and foremost, keeping Venice in the Holy League at a time when its people were starving and the Turks had all the grain. The combined forces of the pope, the Venetians, the Genoese, and Charles V had taken the fort of Castelnuovo in the fall of 1538 from the Turks, hoping to use it to launch future operations; but the emperor had heard no news of the fort's security all summer. One of Mendoza's first reports to Cobos and the emperor carried the tragic news that Castelnuovo had fallen to Charles's archenemy Barbarossa. Mendoza saw the Venetians as the true culprits, for he reported that they had made a unilateral treaty with the Turks, had refused to call up the League's armada, and had allowed the Turks to enter the Gulf of Prevesa off Albania. The Venetians, he added, denied all these accusations and gave several ridiculous excuses for the fall of Castelnuovo. Nevertheless, Mendoza recommended to Cobos that Charles also formulate a treaty with the Turks rather than try to fight them alone. Charles would decide to continue alone, and would suffer his first and most bitter military defeat because of this decision. During the summer of 1541, Charles decided to take Algiers from the Turks, thereby seizing the major port for Barbarossa and his fleet in the western Mediterranean. He deployed his fleet, under the command of Andrea Doria, in the Bay of Algiers on 24 October and marched to within gunshot of the city. It looked as if the coming battle would be quick and easy; but that night a gale hit the fleet, destroyed one hundred and fifty ships, and completely soaked the army's gunpowder. The Algerians took advantage of the situation to harrass the Spanish troops and force them to return to the beaches, where three days later they set sail for Spain, having lost twelve thousand men and the hundred and fifty ships. After this disaster, Charles abandoned attempts to control the Mediterranean seaways. In effect, the next victory against the Turks would not take place until the Battle of Lepanto thirty years later.

Mendoza's letters do not concern solely business, however. They also contain gossip about the local politicians and diplomatic rivals, his various illnesses (mostly stomach ailments), and scattered comments about the Oriental art and furniture that he is constantly buying from the Levant trade ships. In August 1540, a new topic appears that will pepper his correspondence for almost a year: "I made love three times here with one of the most beautiful women (*putanas*) in Italy, but before going all the way she stopped me, and explained she was a Jewess and could not do anything with me unless I became a Jew. I, since I was not far from one or the other, told her to make the plans, since there was little that had to be done. Tell me if I should get circumcised; and if it sounds like a good idea to you, and you get to Venice, prepare your foreskin; for the Jewess is so beautiful, it seems to me a very good trade" (Vázquez and Rose, 46). Can Mendoza be serious? The last line seems to imply he is not; and *putana* means whore in Italian. It is hard to believe that a Spanish nobleman would have himself circumcised just so he could go to bed with a Jewess who must by necessity have no family background. Yet Mendoza insists on his planned conversion. A week later he writes Cobos that he has a house on Murano where he can go with his girl friends, "but if the Jewess wanted me to, I would immediately go live in the Synagogue. My Sir, I've never seen a more beautiful nor intelligent Jewess; she is a woman with a lot of head (*que tiene coca*)" (Vázquez and Rose, 49).

In September, Mendoza reports that the relationship is reaching the boiling point, and he may not have to convert: "Los tratos de la judía tornan a bullir, y creo que sin dexar mi lei haremos paz" (Vázquez and Rose, 51). In November, don Diego writes he has still not won over the lady, and in January he begins to have second thoughts: "Yesterday I went into the Jewish Quarter (*Judería*) and saw my Jewess; her house smells like a slave ship, and so I'm losing interest" (Vázquez and Rose, 63). Then in March he refers to her as "doña Talitla" and "la signora ambasatora," followed by a joke that he is saving her so Cobos can enjoy a Jewish virgin ("La guardo para que V. Sᵃ guste virgo judío si acá viniere"), adding that they may also find a Gentile virgin so they will not break the religious laws, because there are some good Christian women; but the poor Ambassador, circumcised *capite*, will follow the laws of Jehovah: "Y el pobre embaxador, circuncidado *capite*, seguirá la instrutión de Jehová" (Vázquez and Rose, 66). For some reason, that is the end of the affair. In May Mendoza bumped against a chair and one of his testicles swelled, became infected, and had to be amputated. He thanks God he has two, but adds: "You can sympathize with the Jewess, since I had her so domesticated that I was not far from resurrecting my grandparents' bones" (Vázquez and Rose, 72). The Jewess does not appear again in don Diego's letters except in a hurried note on 29 January 1542, when Mendoza complains to Cobos: "I have nothing to say but that this is a very wretched life: kidney pains, fear and suspicions, giving audiences before the spies wake up; and with all this Jewesses and the rest are forgotten about" (Vázquez and Rose, 85).

No one knows the identity of this Jewess, nor if Mendoza was joking or serious about the circumcision, the conversion, and the Jewish skeletons in his family tree. If he were serious, it would make a shambles of theories like those of Américo Castro,[16] which ascribe a morbid fear of mixing with Jews to all "honorable" Spaniards of the sixteenth and seventeenth centuries. Mendoza was more than likely joking about the circumcision and conversion, although he was evidently quite enamored of the Jewess, enough at least to visit her in the restricted Jewish ghetto and broadcast freely his relationship with her. Ironically, this is the only amorous relationship that Mendoza had that has documentary evidence to support it. He assuredly visited frequently the Venetian *putane,* for his letters are riddled with references to them. But no records have come to light documenting any other romantic liaison, and there is no evidence that don Diego ever seriously considered marriage to any known woman.

Life in Venice during this period was by no means all love and sex for Mendoza. The French were intriguing continually against Charles's imperial policies, and Mendoza constantly argued cases before the Senate, intrigued with secret allies, and watched for assassins. During the summer of 1541, two French agents were murdered, and blame was put on Mendoza. He was forced to hire bodyguards to protect himself; but even so a number of attempts were made on his life (Vázquez and Rose, 84, 102, 105).

The emperor, meanwhile, had entered into another disastrous war against France. In the summer of 1542 French troops invaded Spain over the Pyrenees and beseiged the citadel of Perpignan. The duke of Alba came to the city's aid with men and supplies, narrowly averting what could well have been the French occupation of Aragon and Navarre, both empty of resident soldiers. The French abandoned the seige in September to protect Paris from a similar invasion by Charles from Germany; and then, after the traditional wintering of the troops, on Easter Monday of 1543 the French routed the imperial forces under the Marqués de Vasto at Cérésole. The final result was the Peace of Crépy in September, where Charles promised to cede by marriage to Francis's son either Milan or Flanders.

Mendoza had opportunities to meet and discuss the war with Charles between May and July 1543, when the emperor was in Italy to enlist Pope Paul's aid against the French. The pope again refused to take sides because he wanted to buy Milan from Charles and cede it to his grandson Ottavio Farnese, who had married Margaret of Austria, Charles's illegimate daughter. Charles wisely refused to sell the territory.

It is also during this time that the Spanish poet Gutierre de Cetina wrote for Mendoza the *Epístola primera: A don Diego Hurtado de Mendoza*.[17] Cetina was accompanying Charles V, and used his epistle to describe the recent assault and seizure of Dura (24 August 1543) as well as the corrupt life at court. But Cetina must have also been in Venice with Mendoza, because he asked for a painting by Titian he saw in Mendoza's house and he sent his regards to Pietro Aretino, who was one of don Diego's closest friends.

Don Diego was also busy during 1543 preparing for a proposed general council of the church in Trent. He met there with the emperor's chancellor, Nicholas Perrenot of Granvelle and Antoine Perrenot, the son (who would soon succeed Cobos as Charles's secretary) to discuss the reform of the clergy; but the meeting lasted only a few days because—due to the Franco-Hispanic War—no one else attended. The various parties involved did not meet again until March 1545, and Mendoza was the emperor's representative. The council dragged on through the spring without any real progress being made. Don Diego returned to Venice in May, but was back in Trent in June to take part in the debates concerning Justification. He became ill and returned to Venice in September, and did not get back to Trent until May of the next year. He remained there until December, when the council broke up because of an outbreak of the plague.

Mendoza was evidently one of the most popular and well-respected scholars at Trent. A letter from Juan Páez de Castro to Jerónimo Zurita describes brilliantly the role Mendoza was playing among the intellectuals at the council:

I have the house full of ever so many of Don Diego's printed books that I want, and manuscripts too, and his sketchbooks. All here believe that Don Diego will climb very high in position after this Council is over, and that His Majesty will make him bishop, and His Holiness, cardinal. Now we understand the *Mechanica* of Aristotle, making great demonstrations. He has it translated into Romance and has written a glossary;[18] I believe I can help him somewhat. Always he says: "Let us study, Señor Joan Páez." He is so good and humane that you can say "Nihil oriturum" [nobody will be born like this], "alias nihil ortun tale" [also nobody has been born such]; his learning is very varied and unusual; he is a great Aristotelian and mathematician; Latin and Greek [scholar]. . . . Nobody is his equal. In short, he is in a class by himself. (Spivakovsky, 132)

This kind of esteem is typical of what most humanists thought of Mendoza, and the list of men with whom he communicated regularly while in Italy constitutes an honor roll of Italian scholarship. The partial register compiled by González Palencia and Mele includes, among others, Pietro Aretino, Giacomo Sadoleto, Benedetto Accolti, Pietro Bembo, Paolo Giovio, Lazaro Bonamico, Giacomo Nardi, Benedetto Varchi, Ludovico Domenichi, Giovanni Guidiccioni, Alessandro Piccolomini, Alessandro Caravia, Anibale Cruceio, Arnaldo Peraxylo Arlenio, Giovanni Tatti, Giovanni Memmo, Paolo Manuzio, Titian, Giorgio Vasari, and Sansovino.

The only person Mendoza did not get along with was his fellow Spaniard Domingo de Soto, a hard-line Thomist who eventually forced his own theory of justification upon the council. Don Diego left no contemporary remarks about Soto, but in 1549 he had occasion to write from Rome about the Dominican, who was then confessor to Charles V: "Tell Monseñor [Granvelle] that the confessor [Soto] doesn't like me because I defended a doctor Herrera in Trent, whom he dishonestly insulted by calling him in the presence of many bishops a heretic, and because I did not help him print at my cost a commentary of his on the *Physics* of Aristotle, and because in the disputes against him and Saint Thomas I always held the part of Averroes (which I would not have done if I knew he was going to be the [emperor's] confessor), and because I know more philosophy than he does. But let him say what he wants, because I am better than him by not being a Jewish convert (*marrano*), as his ancestors were" (Vázquez and Rose, 124).

The letter from Rome is one of many, because don Diego left Venice in December 1546 to become the imperial ambassador to the Vatican. It was a rather sudden move, probably brought on more by his continuous ill health in the wet and cold climates of Trent and Venice than by politics. The alliance between the pope and Charles V had for all intents and purposes ceased to exist, mainly because the emperor had taken papal troops and money to fight the Lutheran heretics in Germany but had used them instead to put down the rebellious princes, at times employing Protestant forces to quell Catholic regions. Also, the pope was bitterly disappointed when Charles appointed Ferrante Gonzaga as the governor of Milan in 1546, for Paul had assumed the duchy would go to his grandson Ottavio Farnese and Charles's daughter Margaret.

Siena was likewise causing problems. The city state was ostensibly a republic, but since the 1520s it had depended on military "protection" and government from the Holy Roman Empire. In 1546, the Sienese had tired of their resident Spanish administrator, don Juan de Luna, and had chased him and his company of soldiers from the city. Charles V quickly persuaded them to agree to a new governor, who was to be none other than Diego Hurtado de Mendoza.

Other problems awaiting don Diego were the attempts by Paul III to sabotage the Council of Trent by moving it permanently to Bologna (where the pope could easily control events and decisions), whence the members had gone when the plague broke out in Trent. The sovereignty of Piombino was another problem. A little port in Tuscany facing the island of Elba, Piombino was an independent state of fourteen hundred citizens ruled by the Appiani family. Charles V decided he needed it for defensive reasons, and had don Diego go personally to Piombino to wrest it from the Appiani and send them into exile. Finally, Florence caused problems. The present ruler, Cosimo I de' Medici, had been recently married to Leonor de Toledo, the daughter of don Pedro de Toledo, viceroy of Naples. Cosimo was supposedly a staunch ally of Charles and the Empire, but events favored his betraying don Diego and the emperor, expanding the boundaries of Florence into neighboring states. These problems and events— Siena, the Council of Trent, Piombino, Parma and Piacenza, Cosimo's machinations, the Imperial ambassadorship to Paul III and later Julius III—became the responsibility of don Diego, who spent the next five years traveling from Rome to Siena to Florence to Bologna to Piombino and back to Rome. The most productive moments of Mendoza's time from 1547 to 1552 were spent in Rome as the papal ambassador. His tenure there is in two parts, with Paul III, who died on 10 November 1549, and with Julius III from 15 March 1550 until 27 July 1552 when don Diego left Rome forever.

Pope Paul III had never been a good friend of Charles V, for their imperialistic designs often conflicted. A case in point is the status of the duchies of Parma and Piacenza, belonging to the papal states, that had become political pawns in 1527 when Charles V took them over after the sack of Rome and did not return them until 1536. In 1545 Paul III gave both states to his degenerate and perverted illegitimate son Pier Luigi Farnese. Charles considered this a gross act of personal gain prohibited by the papal statutes, and he acted in a typically Machiavellian fashion. When in 1546 the Marqués de Vasto died and left the governorship of Milan open, Charles gave the job to Ferrante Gonzaga with the stipulation that he somehow eliminate Pier Luigi from Parma and Piacenza. On 10 September 1547, a group of conspirators broke into Farnese's castle and murdered him. That very day Gonzaga arrived with imperial troops to occupy Piacenza.

Don Diego knew nothing of all this, but it was his task to tell Paul III how his son had died. The news almost killed the pope; but he recovered, accepted Mendoza's claim that Charles was not personally involved, and allowed Ottavio Farnese to rule both Parma and Piacenza as an independent duchy. Paul died before Ottavio Farnese could be officially given the territories, but Pope Julius III went through the ceremonies in 1550. The matter should have ended there, but within a year both the pope and the emperor had second thoughts about giving the territory to the Farneses, and both—at the instigation of don Diego—decided to try to take it back. Ottavio was resolute, however, and in February 1551 he attacked the imperial military bases in Parma and asked Henry II of France for military aid. The war dragged on for over a year. No great battles were fought, but the outcome was a loss for Charles and a win for the French, who again had a sizeable foothold in Italy. In May 1552, Julius III and Ottavio Farnese reached an accord with respect to the states of Parma and Piacenza, and Charles V agreed to it. There really was not much more the emperor could do, because at the time all of his troops were in Germany fighting a losing campaign against Maurice of Saxony, who had rebelled in March.

These matters occupied Mendoza constantly, for it was he who had to persuade Julius III to enter the war against Ottavio. Later, don Diego was accused of instigating the war, perhaps with the intention of claiming the duchy for himself; but he strongly denied this rumor and valiantly defended his role in the matter in a long report sent to Charles V in April 1552 (see the "Instrucción de don Diego Hurtado de Mendoza a Pedro Ximénez, su secretario," in Vázquez and Rose, 323–38).

Another factor in the conflict between Pope Paul III and the emperor was the problem of relocating the Council of Trent. When the cardinals left Trent for Bologna because of the plague, Pope Paul made every effort to hold it in that "papal" city. Trent was an "imperial" town and Paul was justifiably afraid that any council held there would favor Imperial policies. Matters came to a head in December 1547, when Mendoza delivered an official protest before the papal consistory, arguing that Pope Paul was obstructing a church order by refusing to reconvene the council at Trent. His complaint was unheeded, so on 23 January 1548 he made another official protest that was so inflammatory and noteworthy that it was actually printed in pamphlet form and widely distributed.[19] Pope Paul of course paid no attention to this protest either, and the reconvening of the council had to await the accession of Julius III.

During these same years don Diego also had to deal with Piombino. That such a little place could be so important to him is explained in a letter he wrote to Granvelle: "If the Emperor could see Piombino and Monte Argentario and would remember Genoa and Caeta and Livorno at one end and in the middle, and Civitá Vecchia and other rundown ports among some very good ones, and if he could see how they rim the state of Siena, I mean by having Piombino and making a fort at Porto Santo Stefano and having Orbetello, it ties Spain and Naples like a chain; and the fact is that the chain is a gold one" (Vázquez and Rose, 259–60). To assure the little state's fealty, however, don Diego had to go to Piombino to convince Elena Salviati, the reigning member of the Appiani family, to leave. She refused, and don Diego had her forcibly evicted by carrying her out in the chair in which she was sitting. In order to avoid international tensions, the city was put under the protection of the duchy of Florence in 1548, which was a mistake, because Cosimo signed a final agreement in 1552 turning the state over to himself.

Mendoza's true bête noire was Siena. He took command in October 1547 and often resided in the city for months at a time during his five years in central Italy. From all accounts, Mendoza was a good governor and was well liked by the Sienese. But in the summer of 1550 he decided that Siena needed a modern fort. The emperor thought it was a good idea, as long as the castle did not cost too much money; but Cosimo de' Medici was secretly opposed to it because he saw that it would give Charles's foreign overlords an impregnable fortress within his own area of influence. To the south, Pedro de Toledo, viceroy of Naples, opposed it because he feared Mendoza was acquiring too much personal power in Italy. The Sienese were outraged by the whole matter and tried to sabotage the project from the outset. The truth is that don Diego was not very diplomatic with the Sienese. He chose what he considered a rundown area of Siena to put the fort, but that particular hill had the oldest surviving towers on it, ones very similar to those still standing in San Gimignano. Mendoza cavalierly knocked down ten of them and made deep excavations on the hill, discovering to his joy quantities of Roman artifacts which he prudently confiscated and added to his collection (see Vázquez and Rose, 265–66). As the building of the fort progressed throughout 1551, the Sienese became more and more restless. In March 1552, Mendoza went to Rome to participate in the negotiations over Parma. He thought he was leaving a well-ordered and tranquil Siena, but before he could return in July the city revolted against the Spanish and invited the French to protect them. The Spaniards in don Diego's still unfinished castle surrendered on 27 July 1552 and the Sienese completely dismantled in one day the fort that had taken Mendoza twenty months to build.

Don Diego heard rumors of a possible rebellion in mid-July but could not leave Rome until the twenty-seventh because ten days earlier he had had a fist fight with a Roman police officer, and so angered the pope that he refused to see the Spanish ambassador (Vázquez and Rose, 382–85). By the time don Diego settled the issue it was 26 July. He left Rome as quickly as possible in the middle of the night for Siena, completely unaware that he, the imperial ambassador to the Vatican, would never return to Rome. His march to Siena was blocked along the way by French troops, who had seized all the major highways. He finally had to detour the city, taking refuge with Cosimo de' Medici in Florence, who meanwhile had already signed a peace treaty with the French in Siena. Don Diego left Florence at the end of August and made his way north to Germany to explain the disastrous turn of events in Italy. Passing through Orbetello (which he reconquered for the emperor), Piombino (which he had just signed over to Cosimo), Genoa, Milan, and Basel, he reached the emperor's court at Speier in early October 1552, where he saw his master for the first time in ten years. For his twenty-two years of foreign service he was awarded a small sum of money and membership in the order of Alcántara with the title Comendador de las Casas de Badajoz, and given free passage to Spain via Flanders and London. Don Diego was justifiably offended by this slight to his honor and years of service, and wrote a long letter to Philip, Charles's son and the next king of Spain, complaining bitterly about his treatment. The letter ends with the following scathing denunciation of King Charles V:

The reasons why I left were to give an account of my actions to your highness [Philip] because I had no obligations to his majesty [Charles] as a servant, because the ministers said his majesty did not need me anymore, because his majesty excluded me from some posts for which I was named with words improper for him and for me, because it was not right for his majesty to take away my reputation, and even my honor if he could, after having served him for twenty-two years; and, at the time that I expected gratitude and remuneration, to bring me to the point of justifying my actions.

Because his majesty has done to me what a minister would do only with a servant, and that without cause and at the urging of my enemies, for which I am and will live very hurt and grieved perpetually as long as his majesty and I may live, never forgetting the offense he did me. Because his majesty gave me no more favor than what was necessary for him to protect himself from the imputation that the world could give him, these being my excuse and my innocence, and then I had neither the possibility nor the will to follow his majesty.[20]

The Final Years in Spain

Don Diego's return to Spain marks the end of the detailed accounts of his whereabouts and activities, simply because he no longer writes the letters and reports to the emperor as he did while an ambassador in Italy. He returned to Spain by boat and reported to Philip II in November 1553 at the royal palace in Valladolid, leaving thereafter to undergo the religious duties prescribed for a knight of Alcántara—usually a year's residence in a monastery—although the place and the duration of his preparation are unknown. He had evidently finished the rituals by February 1554, when his brother don Bernardino asked him to help prepare the fleet that was to carry Philip II to England for his marriage to Mary Tudor.[21]

For the next three years, however, there are no known records concerning Mendoza's whereabouts. He was probably at court in Valladolid most of the time. In April 1557, he was named supply officer for the royal armada at Laredo, then being prepared by Philip II to invade France. He may have gone with the fleet when it sailed that summer, and may have also been present for the Battle of Saint-Quentin on 10 August, a stupendous victory for Spain that led to the first permanent peace with the French in one hundred years. The resulting Peace of Cateau-Cambrésis in 1559 terminated France's designs on Italy, giving Siena to the duchy of Florence and restoring little Piombino to the Appiani, who had been so gruffly turned out by don Diego in 1548.

In September 1557, don Diego set sail for England with Ruy Gómez de Silva, count of Melito, to visit Mary Tudor; but he only stayed in England for a few days before crossing into France to join the Spanish king. Mendoza disappears again except for some inquisitorial records from September 1559, November 1561, and June 1562, all in Madrid, concerning the case of Bartolomé Carranza, the archbishop of Toledo who was mysteriously accused of heresy and imprisoned for seventeen years. It is also known that in the fall of 1561 don Diego adopted a grandniece of his, Magdalena de Bobadilla. Her correspondence has been preserved and provides valuable insights into her character and the everyday life of the Madrid aristocracy.[22]

Don Diego again vanishes from the public eye until 1567, when he is made the commanding supply officer for a third armada, this time intended to suppress the rebellious Dutch in Flanders. He was living in Loredo most of 1567 and part of 1568. The armada never embarked, however, and by July don Diego had returned to Madrid. Matters in the capital were very tense at that time, because don Carlos, Philip's mad son and sole inheritor to the throne, was on his deathbed. For reasons never completely understood, on 23 July, the day before the demise of the young Carlos, don Diego and Diego de Leyva, the son of Mendoza's old friend Antonio de Leyva, began arguing outside Philip's chambers. Swords were rattled and drawn, but no one was hurt. The noise caused Philip to investigate personally, and the two don Diegos had to take refuge in a church. The king nevertheless had them both arrested. Mendoza was accused of lese majesty and sent to the Castillo de la Mota in Medina del Campo for six long months.

There exist a number of accounts of this quarrel. The most complete occurs in a letter from an Italian ambassador to Cosimo de' Medici:

I must tell Your Excellency of an incident that happened in the palace on the 23rd, the same day the Prince was about to die. Don Diego de Mendoza, the old one, formerly ambassador in Rome, and Don Diego de Leva, natural son of Antonio de Leva, walking about in the hall of the Queen, had a dispute over some poems called *copule* here. There was some doubt about whether Don Diego de Mendoza had written them, and they started quarreling, so much so that by the time they left the hall for the upper corridors, they were so heated that Mendoza drew his dagger, pointing it at Don Diego de Leva who in turn drew his sword against Mendoza, giving him several blows. It was a very great rumpus, and His Majesty heard it and was extraordinarily upset, first because such a thing is unusual in the palace, and second, because under those particular circumstances something worse might have been suspected. Both sought asylum in a church in order to escape justice and to make peace. Nevertheless, at midnight His Majesty ordered two *alcaldes* to get them out of the church and imprison them, and Don Diego de Leva was put in irons and chains. And the other night he ordered [one of] them taken into the fortress of Medina, and the other to Simancas, not without danger to the life of each of them. His Majesty contemplated punishing his guard for having let them escape from the palace, while they should have been arrested or killed. (Spivakovsky, 363)

The couplets in question are sometimes reputed to be "De don Diego de Leyva a don Diego de Mendoza, despidiéndose de Palacio" and "Respuesta de don Diego de Mendoza."[23] There is nothing in the former to warrant a dispute, however, since it is a typical *desengaño* (disillusion) poem describing the corrupt ways at court. Leyva writes don Diego that he is giving up all the foolish pastimes expected of a gallant in the palace: peeping through keyholes, bribing servants and guards, being up early to see the ladies go to mass and up late to sing beneath their balconies, wearing clothes of their colors, and going to church solely to see them.

Mendoza's reply, however, is mordant, countering each of Leyva's complaints about serving ladies with a pointed insult: peeping through keyholes was the only way Leyva could see the ladies, he was too cheap to bribe guards or even have servants, he could not sing well enough for anyone to want to listen to him, he was too poor to buy clothes of his lady's colors, and no one ever did notice him at mass. Mendoza ends by telling Leyva that if he does not want to play the game, he should not complain about the rules ("Yo os quiero aconsejar, / y tomad mi parecer, / que no queráis más trovar, / no os venga en casa a llover" [*OP*, 339]). These are indeed words to quarrel over, for—if they are actually the ones mentioned by the Florentine ambassador—Diego de Leyva would have been justifiably offended by the way Mendoza inverted and parodied the sense of his harmless poem.

Philip released Mendoza in February, but banished him forever to Granada under the custody of his nephew Iñigo Hurtado de Mendoza, to whom don Diego surrendered himself on 17 April 1569. The two following years in the courtier's life were consumed entirely in keeping a close watch on the Morisco rebellion that had broken out on 23 December 1568. A full account of the war and don Diego's role in it is found in chapter 3, on the *Guerra de Granada*. When the war was over, Mendoza, then seventy years old, requested to return to Madrid to settle some accounts concerning his financial dealings in Siena during his tenure as governor from 1547 to 1552. The king granted him permission to return as long as he did not enter the royal palace. Mendoza left Granada in late 1574 and was in Madrid by November.

The next eight months—the last of his life—were evidently spent in relative calm. Extant records indicate that most of his time was dedicated to organizing his immense holding of books and classical artifacts. He also decided about this time to give his personal library and art collection to the new royal library at the Escorial. As early as 1572 Antonio Gracián, who was in charge of the Escorial library, mentioned in a letter that they were preparing a place for Mendoza's books (González Palencia and Mele, 2:384), and don Diego comments in various letters upon his attempts to catalog the vast collection.

It was this accumulation of books, art, antiquities, coins, and other classical artifacts for which don Diego was best known among his scholarly countrymen. While don Diego was cataloging his books for the Escorial, Ambrosio de Morales was preparing his *Antigüedades de las ciudades de España,* dedicated to Mendoza. Morales's comments provide a fitting encomium to don Diego's entire humanist career as a student of the classics.

Your lordship gave me also with distinguished liberality all the ancient coins you had from the times of the Romans, with names of the places in Spain they came from, and copies and lists of rare inscriptions. They will help me greatly in what I am going to discuss here, as will be seen in the body of the work. And if I had to look for someone who could best judge what has been examined and discovered in this field, who can make the estimation of this my work better than your lordship who so singularly understands all about Roman antiquities? Having together with this so much and such a particular knowledge of this in Spain, for all those who desire to know and with reason think they know something about them recognize in your lordship a mastery and great excellence in knowing them and having them with much wit, diligence and proven judgment. . . .

And because your lordship with your important assignments resided in various places, and your library was so large in every residence that no one could quickly move it, you took other new codices of the authors you most loved and had them copied, as if you had never had it done before. Thus one finds in your library, now that it is all together, two or three works of some of the same authors underlined and annotated by your hand. Because reading and studying was always the greatest entertainment for your lordship; this was your relaxation from business and relief from work.

From this great love that your lordship had for letters has resulted the singular profit of having, as we have, so much and so many famous Greek authors that before we did not have; since as you had brought from Greece many things by Saints Basil, Gregory Nazianzen, Cyril, and by many excellent authors, all of Archimedes, much of Heron, of Appian of Alexandria and of others. And the way of having them brought is another singular deed, because having your lordship sent to the Grand Turk Soliman freely and without any ransom a captive of yours, that great lord requested you to ask for whatever you might desire. Then your lordship asked him for two things very worthy of your largesse and love of letters. You asked him for a shipment of wheat for the Venetians, who were suffering much hunger at that time, and any books that he had in Greek. Thus, after having given a very abundant shipment of wheat, he sent your lordship six boxes full of books and, more truly, full of inestimable treasures of wisdom.[24]

In August, the foot in which Mendoza had had circulatory problems for years finally became infected and contracted gangrene. On the tenth of the month he had to have it amputated. Realizing the end was near, he wrote a last will and testament in which he bequeathed all his worldly belongings to King Philip II as payment for any outstanding bills accrued over the years, stating: "Because I have accounts with the king our master, about which he has some doubts, although the king very well understands that I am not short; to clear my conscience and my loyalty, I make his majesty my universal heir and ask him to name an executor of this my inventory, whom I order to fulfill it to the letter, for there is more than enough property."[25] On 13 August 1575,[26] the last great Spanish humanist passed away.

The principal reaction to don Diego's death concerned his library. On 9 August, a courtier had written Antonio Gracián to tell him don Diego was dying, "so you should tell his majesty that it is up in the air about what he is planning to do with his library, for since the will is closed I haven't been able to know what to do. I saw many books there and many people, and it is possible—and even without it being possible—that when one should want to get the library there won't be one, and therefore it would be a good idea to have some plan; and his majesty could do this as one who has good plans, and you yourself. Advise me immediately, because I would regret the loss of even one page of paper of those that he has."[27] Philip II personally responded that Antonio de Padilla and Francisco Gutiérrez de Cuéllar should take charge of the library. Evidently Gracián himself oversaw the cataloging and transferral of the library. On 9 September he wrote Diego Guzmán de Silva that "after I receive and organize all of don Diego de Mendoza's library I will make a general list of all those that go to his majesty, and I will publish it, because I think it will be a thing to see wherever it appears."[28] The inventory was completed by March, and the books were sent over to the Escorial in June.

The catalog of Mendoza's library (appendix 119 in González Palencia and Mele, 2:481–564) surprises the modern reader more for what it lacks than for what it has. All the Greek and Roman writers are there, especially Aristotle, as well as scores of contemporary studies on the classics. Mendoza also had a nice collection of the Italian classics (Petrarch, Boccaccio, Dante), but there are few books in Spanish, and no Spanish literature at all. In fact, 90 percent of all the works are in Latin or Greek. It is, in other words, the library of a Renaissance humanist, a true European classical scholar. The library reflects poorly if at all the literary background and friendships that Mendoza must have had with the Spanish vernacular tradition during the reign of Charles V, and therefore is somewhat a contradiction to Mendoza's own writings, which were almost entirely in Spanish.

Chapter Two
Mendoza's Poetic Works

Diego Hurtado de Mendoza's poetry was not formally published until 1610, when Fray Juan Díaz Hidalgo did a fairly complete edition in Madrid. By then the courtier's fame as a collector of books and artifacts had passed and he was well-known in Spanish literary circles for two other reasons: as a close ally of Boscán and Garcilaso in the literary war over the introduction of Italianate meters; and, paradoxically, as a good writer of *coplas*, or traditional poetry in *redondilla* verse. Mendoza's friendship with Boscán and Garcilaso was documented in 1543 when don Diego's epistle to Boscán was published with Boscán's reply in *Las obras de Boscán y algunas de Garcilaso de la Vega*, and again in 1553, when the Venetian printer Alonso de Ulloa published along with Boscán's and Garcilaso's works the infamous *Censure of Spanish Poets Who Write with Italian Meters* by Cristóbal de Castillejo. Ulloa's edition carried as well the second piece of poetry by Mendoza to appear in print, his "Fábula de Adonis, Hipómenes y Atalanta," evidently included as a companion piece to Boscán's *Historia de Leandro y Hero*.

Castillejo's sonnet is as follows: "Italian and Latin muses, people from such foreign parts, such new and beautiful carnations, how have you gotten to our Spain? Who brought you to be neighbors of the Tajo, of its mountains and fields? Or who is he who guides and accompanies you through such strange lands of pilgrimage?—Don Diego de Mendoza and Garcilaso brought us, and Boscán and Luis de Haro by order and protection of the God Apollo. Death carried two of them slowly by, Sulieman another, and only don Diego remains to succor us, but he alone is enough."[1] Mendoza is also a member of this group in the *Miscelánea* of Luis Zapata who, when registering "the good canonized writers," lists, among others, "the excellent gentlemen about whom today so much fresh ink is spilled and will be spilled always, Boscán and Garcilaso; don Diego de Mendoza. . . ."[2] Finally, Hernando de Hoces notes about the same time "so many, as those who today have vowed to imitate to the letter this Italian verse, as in all other things; given the fact that it is unjust for anyone to

condemn as bad the verses that don Diego de Mendoza, the secretary
Gonzalo Pérez, don Juan de Coloma, Garcilaso de la Vega, Juan Boscán, and many other learned persons have approved as good."[3]

Despite Mendoza's close alliance with the Italianate style, it was his
traditional Castilian verses that were most prized by posterity. Juan
Fernández de Velasco said of Mendoza's poetry: "His *redondillas* are a
thing that have no equal"; and Lope de Vega asked: "What can outdo
a *redondilla* of Garci Sánchez or don Diego de Mendoza?"[4] Tomás Tamayo de Vargas noted: "The witty knight don Diego de Mendoza,
what did he wish to say that he couldn't in his Castilian *coplas?*"[5] So,
ironically, although Mendoza was best known as a defender of the
new Italianate style, his finest poetry was thought to be his Castilian
redondillas.

The most telling statement from a contemporary of Mendoza is
that of Fernando de Herrera in his annotations to Garcilaso's poetry:

Don Diego de Mendoza found and used his conceits, which describe the
sound and all its perturbations, with more spirit than care; and he achieved
with novelty what he always attempted, which was to separate himself from
the common path of the other poets; and satisfied with it he forgot the other
things, because, since he had spirit and erudition and an abundance of sentiment in all that he wrote, if he had wanted to make use of the purity and
elegance of his language and compose his verses with number and softness,
we would not have to be envious of better ones in other foreign languages.
And one cannot leave off conceding that when he took care in what he wrote,
no one could better him, but since he wrote merely to occupy his idle time
or to free his soul from other bothersome cares, thereby the greatness of sentiments and considerations and the natural wit and flair of his verses turn
him, as I have said, from the mass of common poetry.[6]

Mendoza was also famous for his burlesque and satirical poetry, so
famous, in fact, that Fray Juan Díaz Hidalgo felt it necessary to apol-
ogize for not including any of it in his 1610 edition of don Diego's
poetry: "In his comic poems (not included here for reasons of deco-
rum) he demonstrated wit and elegance, being satirical without harm-
ing anyone, mixing the entertaining and the profitable. "The
Carrot," "The Flea," "The Gray Hair," and other burlesque poems
that he composed for his own pleasure or for his friends have not been
printed so as not to contravene the seriousness of such a famous poet;
and for this reason, those poems will be more esteemed by he who
has them and knows them, since they will not be so accessible."[7]

These last lines are a virtual invitation to the reader to search out Mendoza's burlesque poetry, since Hidalgo reports that they are rare items.

A poem with the title"Elegía de la pulga" has also been attributed to Gutierre de Cetina, and Adolfo de Castro published it under Cetina's name in the *BAE* volume on lyric poets (32:47). Cetina writes an apostrophe-epitaph to a flea who has succeeded in biting the breast of his lady. Cetina and Mendoza did not borrow from each other, however; the slight similarities between their poems are due to their utilizing the same source, Lodovico Dolce's "Capitolo del pulce." Mendoza, in fact, acknowledges his source in the first verses, writing that the poem is a translation and elaboration of a Venetian fantasy ("traducida / de cierta Veneciana fantasía" [*OP*, 450]). Don Diego's version begins with an apostrophe to the flea and describes how the little animal can cause even the most circumspect and prudent person to writhe in agony and hop in desperation. Nevertheless, don Diego would like to be a flea so he could crawl under his lady's clothes and explore every part of her body. He could watch her undress and go to bed; and then, when all the servants had gone, turn back into a man to proposition his beloved. If she refuses him, he could turn back into a flea to torment her with his bites in the very places he earlier had wanted to give her pleasure.

The subject matter of Mendoza's "La zanahoria" can be imagined. It is a poem in praise of the carrot's many virtues and medicinal properties, all of which can be applied as well to the virile member. Aristotle, Plato, Virgil, and Homer should have extolled it, because it is sweet, hard, round, and long; it seems cold but is hot; it is good raw, boiled, roasted, or fried; it has no shell, seeds, or pits; and it can be enjoyed any time of the year. The carrot is especially good for lovers, because it prevents melancholy; and it is of more benefit to them than words, or gestures, or acts of devotion.

The third poem mentioned by Juan Díaz Hidalgo is "A una señora que le envió una cana." Mendoza received a gray hair from a lady and wonders from where it came, because it is too short to be from her head and too thick and stiff to be from her pubic area. If it is from the latter, he would trade all his gray hairs to see its place of origin. On the other hand, he doubts a gray hair could come from such a fresh and verdant field, although its thickness proves it was from a well watered plot of land. If it was found by candlelight, it was because it stood out against the dark background, and if by sunlight, because the sun very rarely had the opportunity to shine on its dwelling place.

Knapp includes other burlesque poems in his volume (*OP*, 433–78) besides the ones mentioned by Hidalgo, although none of them are undisputedly by Mendoza. The two most famous of these others are "En loor del cuerno" (In praise of the horn of cuckoldry) and "Fábula del cangrejo" (The story of the crab). The first is an encomium of horns, especially those worn by men. The burlesque section is a tale about a painter who in a dream met the devil and asked for something to keep his wife from deceiving him. The devil replied that when he awoke he would find a ring around his finger, and if he wore it always his wife would remain faithful.

> Y el pintor despertó despavorido.
>   Y acordándosele de lo soñado,
> se fue a tentar el dedo por ventura
> a ver si era verdad lo que ha pasado.
>   Y halló la mano puesta en la natura
> de su mujer, y dentro el dedo todo,
> y allí conoció claro su locura.
>
> (*OP*, 469)

"La fábula del cangrejo" is somewhat like Boccaccio's devil in the hole. The demigoddess Glauca experienced the misfortune of having a little crab crawl into the most feminine part of her body, and no one could get the animal out. A young man passed by about this time, and they called to him for help. Seeing the area in question, he pulled out his surgical instrument (*la tienta*), went after the crab with it, and soon chased the little creature from its hiding place. When the young man was about to leave, Glauca begged her mother to let him stay, because the crab had given birth to a thousand others. Her mother therefore arranged for the two to marry so the new husband could ferret out the crabs that remained.

Finally, there is the following sonnet that, while not original, since it has versions in almost every European language, is perhaps the most memorable of the burlesque poems attributed to Mendoza:

> Dentro de un santo templo un hombre honrado
> con grande devoción rezando estaba;
> sus ojos hechos fuentes, enviaba
> mil suspiros del pecho apasionado.
>   Despues que por gran rato hubo besado

> las religiosas cuentas que llevaba,
> con ellas el buen hombre se tocaba
> los ojos, boca, sienes y costado.
>   Creció la devoción, y pretendiendo
> besar el suelo al fin, porque creía
> que mayor humildad en esto encierra,
>   lugar pide a una vieja; ella, volviendo,
> el salvo-honor le muestra, y le decía:
> —Besad aquí, Señor, que todo es tierra.
>
>   (*OP*, 441)

Within a holy temple an honorable man was praying with great devotion: his eyes were fountains, he sent impassioned sighs from his chest. After having kissed the religious articles he had brought, he touched his eyes, mouth, temples, and chest with them. His devotion increased; and, finally intending to kiss the floor, because he believed that act held the greatest humility, he asks an old woman for some room; she, turning around, shows him her fundament and said: kiss here, my lord, for it's all earth.

The Courtly Love Poetry

The vast majority of Diego Hurtado de Mendoza's poetic corpus is perhaps regrettably not risqué, but is love poetry in the tradition of the medieval and early Renaissance Castilian *cancioneros*.[8] A large amount of love poetry is written in the typically Spanish *redondilla, quintilla,* and *villancico* forms; but love also comprises the subject matter of almost all the sonnets, many of the *epístolas,* and all of the *canciones* in the Italianate *canzone* verse form. Although the content and psychological tone of this poetry is the least innovative of Mendoza's work, its variety and breadth make don Diego a master of the philosophy of courtly love. Evidently, Mendoza wanted his poetic collection to be known as a spectrum of the courtly expression, for in the Paris autograph manuscript he initiated his verses with a poem similar to Petrarch's and Boscán's initial sonnets in their volumes of poetry. The *locus classicus* is a lyric by Catullus that begins "Quio dono lepidum novum libellum."

Malcolm C. Batchelor has argued that Mendoza also intended for his verses to form a sequence, as did those of Petrarch and Boscán:

Except for two epigrams, four sonnets, and the epitaph which don Diego wrote for his unfortunate sister, doña María de Pachecho [*sic*], the remaining poems are addressed to doña Marina or to Marfira, or at least may be interpreted in such a way that all together they form a *cancionero* for which the sonnet, "Libro, pues que vas ante quien puede," serves as a prologue. The sonnets (including those which show a Petrarchist derivation or the direct inspiration of Ausias March), the eclogues and the *epístolas* seem to follow an ordered pattern, in which themes dealing with time, the lover's sorrow, the lady's indifference are connected by a major sustaining theme of separation and recollection from afar.[9]

This hypothesis is untenable. The order of the poems in the auto-graph manuscript does not warrant the attribution of a story line, since much extraneous material is intercalated and no specific develop-ment of a love relationship is ever alluded to; nor does the 1610 *princeps* substantiate the thesis, for there the order of poems is entirely different.

Batchelor follows earlier scholars in assigning to doña Marina de Aragón the role of the recipient of all the love poetry.[10] This girl was the daughter of don Alonso de Aragón y Gurrea, fifth count of Riba-gorza, and of doña Ana Sarmiento de Ulloa, the count's third wife. She was born in 1523 and served as a lady-in-waiting to Empress Isa-bel. By the spring or early summer of 1549 she was dead, at the age of twenty-six. Mendoza was therefore already nineteen years old when doña Marina was born and forty-five when she died. Is it at all possi-ble for him to have written love poems to a lass who would have still been in the cradle when he began composing them? Definitely not. It is not improbable that Mendoza could have dedicated to this partic-ular person the poetry in which her name appears (sonnet 5, *Epístolas* 5 and 6, the elegy, and "Fabula de Adonis, Hipómenes y Atalanta"), since all of these pieces would have been composed at least after 1539 and probably in 1541 (see González Palencia and Mele, 1:247); but it is impossible for doña Marina to be the beloved described in the courtly love poetry, where her name does not appear, although that of "Marfira" does. It would be prudent here not to make the mistake of attributing real feelings to courtly poetry, as was done with the spurious love of Garcilaso for Isabel Freire,[11] and to follow the sound advice of Morel-Fatio to leave the question of any relationship be-tween don Diego and doña Marina de Aragón on the sidelines of liter-ary scholarship.[12]

Mendoza's introductory sonnet is a fitting beginning to his poetic corpus, for it is one of his best poems, as Mitchell D. Triwedi has demonstrated:[13]

Libro, pues que vas ante quien puede
quitar y poner leyes a su mando,
ten cuenta con Damón, allá llegando,
aunque Marfira más te mande y vede.
  Sepas muy bien contar cuanto sucede
después que Damón vive lamentando;
y pues él va contigo allá cantando,
Marfira te oirá, que se lo debe.
  En tanto quedo yo con tal recelo
cual con fortuna brava suele estar,
echando el hierro al mar, el marinero,
  lleno de afán y temeroso celo
si afierra el hierro de donde esperar
la salud debe que a Damón espero.

                                        (*OP, I*)

Book, since you will present yourself to she who can impose and retract laws at her command, take account of Damón by going there, even if Marfira stops you and bans your entrance. You know very well how to relate all that happens, now that Damón lives in lamentation; and since he goes with you there in song, Marfira will hear you, for she owes it to him. Meanwhile, I remain with the same fear as one who usually lives with angry fortune, like the mariner who throws his anchor into the sea, filled with anxiety and timorous fervor about whether the anchor will hold, where Damón can hope for the safety that I expect for him.

As Triwedi notes, the poem is decidedly courtly, stressing suffering, anxiety, sickness, and the expectation of the bestowal of a favor.[14] The poem has two basic parts: the octet, in which the book is given the role of a messenger or intermediary on behalf of the fictional speaker Damón, and the sestet, which describes the state of mind of the poet (not Damón) as he awaits the reply. The sonnet is thus a hidden apostrophe—since it is ostensibly directed to a book but really directed to Marfira (which is also a disguised name)—from a hidden speaker—since it is Damón who speaks in the book rather than Mendoza. The true speaker is further removed from the true receiver by the introduction of a mariner ("el marinero") in the sestet as a simile for the apprehension that Mendoza feels for Damón ("la salud que *a Damón* espero"). One thus reads a sonnet written to a book (that contains the sonnet) that is intended for Marfira (a pseudonym for don Diego's lady) in which Damón (a pseudonym for don Diego) complains of his unrequited love. The poet also speaks in the sonnet, but only to compare himself to a metaphorical sailor and to Damón, whose safety (the mariner's "salud") and health (Damón's "salud") he hopes for. The poem is indeed sophisticated and can easily compete in artistic merit with those by Mendoza's contemporaries.

The bulk of Mendoza's love poetry develops the many facets of the courtly love psychology glimpsed in the introductory sonnet. The typical topoi of the genre that don Diego employs are the same as those outlined by Otis H. Green[15] and others for the courtly stance: *la belle dame sans merci; service d'amour* and *Fraundienst und Vassalität; la superiorité de la dame* and *Frauverehrung; amor purus* and *fin' amors; éloignement* and *amour lointain; fenhedor; amant désespéré; heroes.* These terms delineate the requisites for a courtly affair. In laymen's language, the lover must subject himself in vassalage *(Vassalität)* to his lady, venerate her *(Frauverehrung),* and give her total service *(service d'amour)* as if she were a truly superior being *(la superiorité de la dame).* The passion must also be a secret one in which the adorer conceals his feelings from others *(fenhedor),* and the lover must worship the lady from afar *(amour lointain),* which is best accomplished when the two are separated by a great distance *(éloignement).* Further, the lady will invariably be disdainful and haughty, becoming a *belle dame sans merci* for the suffering paramour. This in turns makes the lover an *amant désespéré,* who will contemplate death as the only remedy for her rejection of him. Because of the absolute service and adoration of the lover and the cruelty and disdain of the beloved, the passion becomes an unfulfilled *amor purus* that increases from the unsatisfied ardor of the man's erotic imagination rather than from satisfaction of the appetites. The constant increase of this fierce heat in the body in turn causes the lover's illness known as *heroes,* characterized by sadness, loss of memory, an overwrought imagination, the desire to be alone, and a physical wasting away of the flesh. Paradoxically, however, these intense physical and emotional maladies purge the body and soul of all the functional capacities that do not relate directly to adoration of the lady, thereby cleansing the lover and creating in him a refined love *(fin' amors)* in which the dross has been burned away by reduction of the base elements in the crucible of Eros. The whole process thus becomes a kind of religion *(religio amoris)* in which the lover worships his lady at the altar of Love.

Mendoza describes all these various states of courtly love in his poetry, although the step-by-step process is never specifically outlined. The predominant motifs are the absence of the lover, his silence, the incredible suffering he experiences (although often joyfully), and a constant desire for death. This content, however, has absolutely nothing to do with the poetic form. The same language and style appears in sonnets, Italianate *canciones,* and tercets as often as it does in the Castilian *redondillas, quintillas, endechas,* and *villancicos.*[16]

A random example of how Mendoza poeticizes the courtly topoi is his *Carta,* no. 4: "Quejándose de su dama y de sus enemigos, que son causa de que ella le olvide." The poem begins

> Gloria y descanso perdido,
> puesto que, si gloria tuve,
> no fue por el bien que hube,
> sino de haber bien servido,
>   ya que os perdí por mi suerte,
> y he de callar y sufrillo,
> adoro y beso el cuchillo
> que me viene a dar la muerte.
> ....
>   Siempre bendigo la hora,
> cuando alegre, cuando triste,
> que por tuyo me quisiste,
> y te adoré por señora;
>   pues vengo a ser envidiado
> y corrido sin por qué,
> como mártir de tu fe,
> en mi sangre confirmado.
>   Persecuciones y penas
> son para mí gran vitoria,
> pues con sola tu memoria
> las sufro y tengo por buenas.
> ....
>   Servir callando y sufriendo
> sólo soy el que lo puede,
> y ya que más no me quede,
> quedarme he a morir sirviendo.
>   (*OP,* 292–95)

Lost glory and rest, since, if I had glory, it was not for any benefit I received but for having served well. Now that it is my fate to lose you and I have to be silent and suffer, I adore and kiss the knife that comes to give me death. . . . I always bless the hour when happily and when sadly I believed you loved me, and I adored you as my lady; now I have become the object of envy and anger without any explanation, like a martyr to your faith con-

firmed in my blood. Persecutions and pain are for me a great victory, since
with only your memory I suffer them and hold them as good things. . . .
To serve by being silent and suffering, I am only being what I can be, and
now that nothing else remains for me, it only remains for me to die serving
you.

*El bein servido, callar y sufrillo, adorar y besar el cuchillo, la muerte,
mártir de la fe, persecuciones y penas, morir sirviendo:* all this is the language of love for the courtly poets. Mendoza restates it hundreds of
times. He has entire poems with titles such as "A la desesperación de
su amor" (To his love's desperation), "A su pensamiento desfavore-
cido" (To his unrequited love), "Al silencio de sus quejas" (To the
silence of his complaints), "Redondillas de pie quebrado" in which
every strophe ends with "sufro y callo," "A su dama estando ausente"
(To his absent lady), "Viéndose sujeto al amor" (Seeing himself captured by love), and a section of eight poems in *redondillas* and *quintillas* that all begin with either the word *cuidados* (cares) or *pesares*
(sorrows).

The value of service is specifically extolled in an intricate *villancico:*

> Pues no me vale servir,
> amar ni bien querer,
> ¿qué me ha de valer?
>   Servicios bien empleados,
> aunque mal agradecidos,
> tal soy yo, que vais perdidos
> por donde otros van ganados;
>   que, mi ventura menguada
> y enemiga de mi bien
> os ha traído ante quien
> poco es mucho, y mucho nada.
>   Pues al fin de la jornada
> y tiempo del merecer,
> el servir no vale nada,
> el amar ¿qué ha de valer?
>
>   (*OP,* 410)

Since service does me no good, what good will it do me to love or desire
well? Well-employed services, although poorly appreciated, such am I that
you are lost where others are gained; for my waning fortune, the enemy of
my welfare, has brought you before she for whom little is much and much
is nothing. Since at the end of the time and working period for meriting
favor, if service is worth nothing, what is love worth?

Other *redondillas* connect the silence and suffering to disdain and death:

> Del mal a que estoy sujeto,
> tanto vivo atormentado,
> que el corazón ha llorado
> sus lágrimas en secreto.
> Tanto ha llegado a sentir
> su riguroso desdén,
> que ha llegado a estarme bien
> el desearme morir.
> Y con ser tal mi dolor,
> aquella ingrata, homicida,
> para animarme la vida
> aun no me ha dado un favor.
> Bella Filis, llegó el día
> en que ha llegado mi suerte,
> que vengo a buscar la muerte,
> y hallar la muerte querría.
> (*OP*, 372–73)

From the infirmity to which I am subject, I live so tormented, that the heart has cried tears in secret. It has come to feel her rigorous disdain so much that it has become a good thing for me to desire death. And with my pain being so much, that ingrate, that murderess, has not even given me a boon in order to urge me to live. Beautiful Filis, the day has arrived in which my fate has reached the point that I come to look for death, and I would desire to find death.

Yet the result of this suffering and pain, this silent adoration and martyrdom, is not death at all, but *fin' amors,* the refined pure love that remains unsullied by evil or lascivious thoughts and that will live forever, even after the physical body has turned to dust. Quevedo described it in his famous sonnet "Amor constante más allá de la muerte" ("Cerrar podrá mis ojos la postrera"). Mendoza portrays it in sonnet 26:

> Salid, lágrimas mías, ya cansadas
> de estar en mi paciencia detenidas;
> y siendo por mis pechos esparcidas,
> serán mis penas tristes mitigadas.
> De mil suspiros vais acompañadas,
> y por tan gran razón seréis vertidas,

que si mi vida dura por mil vidas,
jamás espero veros acabadas.
   Y si después, llegado el final día,
do por la muerte dejaré de veros,
hállase algún lugar mi fantasía,
   el alma, que aun en muerte ha de quereros,
a solas sin el cuerpo lloraría
lo que en vida ha llorado sin moveros.

                                        (*OP,* 18)

Leave, my tears, now tired of being detained by my patience; for by being scattered on my breast, my sad pain will be mitigated. You go accompanied by a thousand sighs, and you are being shed for such a great reason, that if my life should last a thousand lives I would never expect to see you ended. And if afterward, when the final day arrives where I will stop seeking you because of death, my fantasy will find some way. The soul, that even in death will continue to adore you, alone without the body, will cry what in life it has cried without moving you.

This indeed is a total love, one that absorbs the poet's complete being. Mendoza describes it with a sincerity that is believable, if wholly unjustified by events in his life; for the poetry is totally literary, an exercise in the art of writing rather than the expression of personal experience.

The vast majority of Mendoza's love poetry remains tied to the long tradition of the courtly poetics of suffering, service, absence, disdain, and desperation. In effect, his poetic corpus has only one courtly poem[17] that is positive and radiant in the expression of love, although it too displays the total surrender of the lover to his lady:

Sonnet 28

   Ora en la dulce ciencia embebecido,
ora en el uso de la ardiente espada,
ora con la mano y el sentido
puesto en seguir la caza levantada;
   ora el pesado cuerpo esté dormido,
ora el ánima atenta y desvelada,
siempre en el corazón tendré esculpido
tu ser y hermosura entretallada.
   Entre gentes extrañas, do se encierra
el sol fuera del mundo y se desvía,
duraré y permaneceré desta arte.

En el mar, en el cielo, so la tierra
contemplaré la gloria de aquel día
que mi vista figura en toda parte.

(*OP,* 19)

Whether dedicated to sweet science or to use of the burning sword, or with my hand and my senses given to follow the chase of the hunt; whether the heavy body is asleep, or the soul awake and alert, my heart will always have sculpted upon it your being and carved into it your beauty. Among foreign peoples, where the sun retreats from the world and alters its course, I will keep and retain always this love. Upon the sea and in the sky and on the earth and in every part of the world I will contemplate the glory of that day when my eyes saw you.

The first six lines are similar to the preliminary verses of Garcilaso's *Egloga* I ("El dulce lamentar de dos pastores") in the use of *ora / ora / ora,* and *ora / ora / siempre,* especially since the first three references are to the same gentlemanly pursuits of writing, warring, and hunting that Garcilaso describes. The second quatrain universalizes the poet's devotion by having it occupy *all* his time (*dormido* and also *atenta y desvelada*) and *all* his being (*cuerpo* and also *ánima*) for always (*siempre*). Mendoza also ingeniously parallels his own body/soul devotion to the lady's being/beauty (*ser/hermosura*) that he has sculpted and carved respectively into his heart. The sestet further extends the completeness of the poet's love by adding *everywhere (mar, cielo, tierra, toda parte)* and the reiterated statement of permanence (*duraré y permaneceré);* and the placing of "en toda parte" at the end of the sonnet gives final emphasis to the entirety of the poet's adoration. It is a brilliantly measured and well-balanced sonnet that shows how Mendoza, when he wished, could express the Renaissance spirit permeating Spanish thought in the first half of the sixteenth century.

The Poetry of Classical Inspiration

Although the bulk of Diego Hurtado de Mendoza's verse is courtly love poetry, some of his best poems are in imitation of classical models, particularly the *Greek Anthology,* Ovid, Horace, Claudian, and Virgil. His borrowings range from literal translations to free renditions of the original, although most of the pieces are what today would be considered paraphrases.[18] Yet don Diego are evidently aware of the problems and outcomes involved in plagiarizing the classics.

According to the seventeenth-century poet Esteban Manuel de Villegas, it was Mendoza—and not Cervantes—who compared translations to "tapestries seen from the back, where the figures were outlined, but full of knots and threads."[19]

Mendoza's longest and most praised work is in this group.[20] It is a long poem entitled "Fábula de Adonis, Hipómenes y Atalanta," published in Venice in 1553 by Alonso de Ulloa along with the works of Juan Boscán and Garcilaso de la Vega. The majority of Mendoza's "Fábula" is taken from Ovid's *The Metamorphoses*, book 10, verses 425–739. The subject matter of both is in three basic parts: the love of Venus and Adonis, the story of Atalanta and Hippomenes, and the death and metamorphosis of Adonis. Mendoza's poem, written in royal octaves rhyming *ababab cc*, has the following format: the proposition (1), the dedication to doña Marina de Aragón (2–4), the birth and youth of Adonis (5–15), the affair between Adonis and Venus (16–42), Venus's warning concerning fierce beasts, exemplified by the story of Atalanta and Hippomenes (43–94), and the death and metamorphosis of Adonis (95–103). The distribution of these parts in Ovid is almost identical.

Mendoza also borrowed from Claudian, Lucretius, and Virgil. From the first he took several passages from the *Epithalamium Dictum Palladis et Celerinae* for the description of Venus (16–18: "En la Arabia es fama que cansada / . . . / y su hermoso cuerpo descubierto"). He also borrowed two strophes from Claudian's *De Nuptiis Honorii et Mariae* for his strophes 30–31 ("La libertad andaba desceñida, / . . . / se vían por la yerba deleitosa"). The borrowings from Lucretius and Virgil are minor in comparison to these.[21]

The first section of the "Fábula" is a delightful journey into the pagan classical world. The obligatory propositional strophe summarizes succinctly the argument:

> El tierno pecho de cruel herida
> por la dura salvaje fiera abierto;
> la madre del amor toda afligida,
> que con lágrimas baña el joven muerto;
> y tú, virgen, de Hipómenes vencida
> entre gloria dudosa y miedo cierto:
> seréis el argumento desta historia,
> que presente hará vuestra memoria.
>
> (*OP*, 233)

The tender breast, opened with a cruel wound by the harsh savage beast, the mother of love all grief-stricken, who bathes the dead youth with tears; and you, virgin, conquered by Hippomenes, between doubtful glory and certain dread, will be the subjects of this story, which will bring back the memory of you.

Then follow three strophes dedicated to doña Marina de Aragón, very similar to those written by Garcilaso for his ecologues. The story proper begins with the fourth strophe ("En la mar, donde el sol resplandecer"), in which appears a classical description of the dawn. It introduces Myrrha, who has fled from her home after having secretly slept with her father Cinyras and become pregnant by him. She bewails her fate, and God answers her supplications by turning her into the Myrrh tree. The child in her womb remains alive, and after a normal time is delivered from the tree by Lucina, the goddess of childbirth. She gives him to the nymphs to raise, and they name him Adonis the Beautiful.

The next section (strophes 15–42), which intercalates Claudian's verses into Ovid's tale, describes the beauty of Venus, her falling in love with Adonis when she is accidentally scratched by one of Cupid's arrows, and her initial persuasions to prevent him from hunting wild beasts. In this last section, Mendoza aids the reader's comprehension of Ovid's story by explaining more fully why the savage animals detest Venus:

> Ningún animal hay que tanto mueva
> y altere contra sí mi condición
> como el crudo león y matador,
> por haber sido ingrato a mí y a Amor.
> ....
> Soy contenta—dijo ella—de decir
> cuán mal agradecieron mi piedad,
> contándote el milagro y caso extraño
> que a mí causó vergüenza y a ellos daño.
> (*OP,* 242–43)

There are no animals that change and alter their temperament against me like the cruel and damaging lion, for having been ungrateful to me and Love. . . . I am content, she said, to tell how badly they repaid my piety by telling you about the miraculous and strange case that gave me vengeance and them harm.

In Ovid's version Venus only reports without elaboration that she will tell the story about why animals fear and hate her.

The body of the "Fábula" (strophes 43–94) is a faithful rendition in Spanish of the tale in *The Metamorphoses*. The only additions to the argument that Mendoza adds are again to give a clearer cause for the events that occur. To justify better Venus's punishment of Hippomenes and Atalanta, don Diego has the goddess say:

> Ni de mí se acordaron al presente,
> ni me adoraron con debido oficio;
> antes menospreciaron mi deidad,
> llevados de soberbia y vanidad.
>   Con subido furor y dura saña,
> (sintiendo el menosprecio que te digo),
> revolví contra ellos fuerza y maña,
> por mostrar nuevo ejemplo de castigo,
> dándoles a entender que quien engaña
> a Dios, le hallará bravo enemigo,
> sin faltarle cruel pena y tormento,
> en que los otros tomen escarmiento.
>   (*OP*, 256–57)

They did not even remember me at the time, nor did they adore me with proper services; on the contrary, they disdained my deity, transported by pride and vanity. With sudden furor and new cruelty, (resenting the disdain about which I told you), I turned against them with force and cunning, to demonstrate a new manner of punishment, making them understand that he who deceives God will find in him a strong enemy who lacks not in cruel pain and torment from which others can take warning.

The finale is also a copy of Ovid's tale, with one strange exception. Whereas the Roman poet ends his song with the transformation of Adonis into the anemone, Mendoza adds that Venus rejected love forever and ascended to the clear light and golden rays of the chaste moon: "Y ella toma de Amor justa venganza, / no llamándose madre del Amor, / antes con rayos de oro y clara lumbre / sigue la casta luna en alta cumbre."[22]

Mendoza also drew heavily from Ovid for the composition of the *Carta en redondillas* "Amor, amor, que consientes," in which he includes the story of Anaxarete from book 14 of *The Metamorphoses*. Garcilaso de la Vega used the same subject matter in an identical way in

his famous "Oda a la flor de Gnido." Mendoza's poem is longer, however, and is a more direct paraphrase of Ovid's tale. Written in *abba*
rhyme, the poem has exactly one hundred strophes. The first fifty are
a courtly love complaint to a lady who does not reward his continual
service. The language and tone are identical to the many other *Cartas*
that Mendoza wrote on the same subject. The last half of the poem is
decidedly different. Because of its source, the section breathes a lyrical
quality not present in the first half, for most of the verses are tran-
scriptions from the Latin.

The tale in Ovid is actually a story within a story, and it is used
in a different context. Ovid interrupts his register of the later kings
of Alba to relate the adventures of Pomona and Vertumnus. Pomona
was a disdainful girl who spent all her time working in her garden.
Vertumnus fell in love with her; and, in order to woo her, disguised
himself as a harvester, a muleteer, a tinker, a pruner, a soldier, a
fisherman, and finally as an old woman. In this last garb he exhorted
Pomona to take a man and used the story of Iphis and Anaxarete as
an example of what may happen to disdainful women, ending with
the persuasive moral: "Now come, my dear, to find yourself less
cold. / This is no season to resist a love; / Let's hope no April frost
stains apple blossoms, / Or rough winds sweep their flowers to de-
cay."[23] After which he stripped off his disguise and everything else,
convincing Pomona by the beauty of his godlike figure to partake of
the delights of love.

Mendoza supplies an introductory stanza—"Aun la memoria es hoy
viva / de Anaxarte . . ." (*OP, 268*)—and then follows Ovid closely,
adding verses from time to time at points where the Roman's version
is idiomatic or too terse. In the original, for example, Iphis only hears
words from his beloved's mouth once, when "as stubborn as a rock
that clings to earth, / She laughed and turned away—and what she
said / Had more contempt than anything she did."[24] Iphis then immediately denounces her disdain and hangs himself at her door. Mendoza gives this passage more verisimilitude by making a typical
lifelong courtly love affair out of it:

> Jamás dobló la cerviz,
> siempre tan dura y uraña
> como piedra en la montaña,
> que aun se traba en su raíz.
> Si alguna ocasión se ofrece

de mostrar con él clemencia,
en ausencia y en presencia
le desdeña y escarnece.
   Y pasa más adelante;
que a tantas obras esquivas
junta palabras altivas,
dichas con fiero semblante.
   A las veces le halaga
y engaña con esperanza,
porque después la mudanza
mayor impresión le haga.
   Detúvolo muchos años
en tormento tan cruel,
que nunca se acordó dél
sino para estos engaños.

                              (*OP,* 270)

She never bent her neck, always so hard and surly like the mountain rock
that even sets roots. If some occasion occurs to offer him clemency, in his
absence and in his presence she disdains and mocks him. And she does worse;
for to so many aloof actions she adds haughty words, spoken with a fierce
semblance. Sometimes she flatters and deceives him with hope, so that afterward her change will make a stronger impression on him. She held him
many years in such cruel torment that she never paid any attention to him
except for these deceits.

This difference between Ovid's light and brief lines and Mendoza's
heavy and long explanations marks the abyss that don Diego tried to
bridge and could not. Although the Spaniard's lines are more easily
understood and establish better causes and motives behind Iphis's sui-
cide, they also are less poetic.

   The same desire to fill out and give more logical explanations for
the participants' actions appears in Iphis's speech, which is a full fifty-
two lines (25 percent of the poem) in Mendoza. The climax of the
Carta, on the other hand, is succinctly and bluntly reported in both
versions, although Mendoza's gives Iphis a Christian burial rather
than a pagan cremation. The Spaniard's finale is, in fact, briefer and
more truncated than is Ovid's, because Mendoza does not include the
Roman's statement that Anaxarete's statue is in Salamis nor the *Carpe
Diem* exortation of Vertumnus that Pomona succumb to her lover's
proffer:

Llevan el desventurado
adonde la madre estaba,
que sospechosa quedaba
deste o semejante hado.
    La cual, después de haber hecho
las obsequias y lloralle,
por la desdichada calle
pasó acompañando el lecho.
    Anaxárete lo oyó
algo más blanda y humana,
y paróse a una ventana
por ver la muerte que dió.
    Dios y su desconfianza
ya la traían turbada,
toda desasosegada
con temores de venganza.
    Y dijo con rostro esquivo,
mas con algun sentimiento:
    ¡Quiero ver su enterramiento,
pues no le quise ver vivo!
    Apenas vio que traían
a Ifis muerto y tendido,
que los ojos y el sentido
sintió que se endurecían,
    y la sangre colorada,
huyendo del claro gesto,
le dejó amarillo presto,
y tornó blanca y helada.
    Ella procuró volverse,
mas los pies se le trabaron,
y todo el cuerpo dejaron
sin fuerzas para moverse.
    Quiso tornar la cabeza;
tampoco pudo hacello,
que la persona y el cuello
era todo de una pieza.
    Y poco a poco muriendo,
fue en viva piedra tornada,
y aun no pareció mudada
según fue dura viviendo.

(*OP*, 273–74)

They carried the unfortunate fellow to his mother, who waited suspecting this kind of fate. She, after having done the funeral rites and cried for him,

went along the unfortunate street with the coffin. Anaxarete saw it, somewhat kinder and more human, and stopped at a window to see the death she
had caused. God and her wariness now disturbed her, all upset with fears of
vengeance. And she said with an aloof demeanor, but with some feeling: "I
wish to see his burial since I refused to see him alive." She hardly saw them
bring Iphis dead and stretched out, when she felt already her eyes and senses
harden; and her red blood, fleeing from her bright features, quickly turned
her yellow and made her white and frozen. She tried to turn around, but her
feet failed her, and her whole body was left without the ability to move. She
tried to turn her head, which she could not do either, for the body and the
neck were all of a piece. And dying little by little, changing into living rock,
she still did not appear altered from what she would be if alive.

Mendoza closes with the verbal irony of Anaxarete wanting to turn
her head and neck and turning into "viva piedra," thereby referring
back to Anaxarete's nature as someone who "jamás dobló la
cerviz, / siempre tan dura y uraña / como piedra en la montaña." In
Ovid's version Anaxarete did not know the funeral was for Iphis and
went running to the window because, in her words, "We'd love to
see a wild and weeping miserable funeral";[25] whereas in Mendoza's account Anaxarete knows it is Iphis and actually feels a little remorse.

   One of Mendoza's most profitable sources of inspiration was the
Greek Anthology, a vast collection of epigrams and short poetry from
the earliest times. The poems in the *Greek Anthology,* also known as
the *Planudean Anthology* because it was compiled in 1301 from earlier
volumes by a Byzantine named Maximus Planudes, are descendants of
inscriptions usually carved or written on some monument or memorial, often as an epitaph to someone. By Roman times, any very
short, pithy poem could serve as an epigram and thus find its way
into the collection, which eventually contained some thirty-seven
hundred Greek epigrams from 700 B.C. to 1000 A.D., as well as
about four hundred Christian poems from the Byzantine period. The
collection reached Italy in 1460, and was immediately popularized.
The first printed version of the *Planudean Anthology,* edited by the
Greek scholar Janus Lascaris, came out in 1494 at the Alopa Press in
Florence, and was reprinted in 1503 by the Aldine Press in Venice.
   According to Irving P. Rothberg,[26] Mendoza incorporated no less
than eight poems from the *Greek Anthology* into his Spanish verse. The
two most famous ones, "A Venus" and "A Lais," direct descendants
from the collection, were long thought to be imitations of epigrams
by Ausonius.[27] "A Venus" comes from poem 16, 174 in the *Planudean Anthology,*[28] and has a long artistic tradition:

Venus se vistió una vez
en hábito de soldado;
París, ya parte y juez,
dijo, de vella espantado:
—Hermosura confirmada
con ningún traje se muda:
¿Véisla cómo vence armada?
Mejor vencerá desnuda.

(*OP*, 430)

Venus dressed up once in a soldier's garb; Paris, now judge and jury, said, astonished when he saw her: no clothes can change confirmed beauty. You see how she conquers armed? She will conquer better naked.

Under the title "Venus Armata" or "Venus Victrix" the theme was used by Poliziano in the poem "In Venerem Armatam" and by Botticelli in his painting *Mars and Venus,* where it plays on the idea that love is war.[29] The other epigram, "A Lais" is a rendition of poem 6.1 in the *Planudean Anthology:*

Laïs, que ya fui hermosa,
este mi espejo consagro
a tí, Venus sacra diosa,
de hermosura milagro.
   Ya yo no le he menester
si no tornas a hacerme,
pues cual fui, no puedo ser,
y cual soy, no quiero verme.

(*OP*, 430)

I, Lais, who was once beautiful, consecrate this my mirror to you, sacred goddess Venus, miracle of beauty. I no longer need it if you do not come to redo me, since as I was I cannot be and as I am I care not to see.

A third epigram by Mendoza, "A los hijos de Pompeo," written in the same *redondilla* couplet with identical style and rhythm, comes from Martial's *Epigrammata* (book 5, 74):[30]

La Asia y la Europa encierra
los dos hijos de Pompeo,
y al padre mató en la tierra
de Egipto el rey Tolomeo.

El mundo todo a tropel
se juntó a dalles cabida;
que para tan gran caída
no bastó una parte dél.

(*OP*, 431)

Asia and Europe enclose Pompey's two sons, and King Ptolemy killed the
father in the land of Egypt. The whole world gathered in a mad rush to give
them room; for such a great downfall one part of the world was not enough.

Three other poems inspired by the *Greek Anthology* are in sonnet
form, while others occur in a long section of *Epístola*, 4 ("Qué hace
el gran señor de los romanos?").[31] Yet another is the poem *A la varie-
dad de la fortuna*.[32] The three sonnets are "A la ribera de la mar sen-
tada," from 7.145 in the *Planudean Anthology*; "El escudo de Aquiles,
que bañado," from 9.115; and "Demócrates, deléitate y bebemos,"
from 9.19. All are decidedly different from the courtly love sonnets
that surround them, indicating thereby their foreign provenance.

Mendoza borrowed from the early Greek poets Pindar and Homer
various passages around which to construct his *Epístola*, 7: "A su her-
mano don Bernardino de Mendoza." After the initial salutation, don
Diego pictures the career of life as a pilgrimage in which the traveler
strays farther and farther from the true path until he finally realizes
his mistake ("hasta que la verdad y el conocido / error a la opinion
muestra y enseña / cómo no hay que fiar en el sentido" [*OP*, 149]).
He then congratulates his brother for following always the proper
path and inserts a passage from Pindar's Olympic Ode I ("No hay
elemento alguno que se iguale / . . . / que por el cielo yermo se desvía"). The poet outlines his fantasy-filled life in Venice, closing with
a twenty-four-line passage that elaborates on a short section in book
24 of *The Iliad*. The two imitated passages fit well into the context
of the epistle and show that Mendoza could be very successful in
blending his own style and thoughts with those of classical writers.

The Moral Epistles

Mendoza utilized material from classical authors for his meditative
verse letters as well. These pieces, of which there are four ("El no

maravillarse hombre de nada"; "Cuántos hay, don Luis, que sobre nada"; "¿Qué hace'l gran señor de los Romanos?"; "Ilustre capitán vitorioso"), are the only poems by Mendoza that reflect what could be called an ethical philosophy. They have been justifiably called "Mendoza's most perfect poems,"[33] for they express a level of intellectual humanism transcending anything else in his poetic corpus.

All four epistles reflect their generic provenance quite well, being decidedly Horatian in that they possess the same characteristics found in Horace's epistles. According to Elias L. Rivers, "the essential elements of this form are meter, a more or less colloquial diction, an epistolary framework, and moralistic subject matter."[34] The meter used by Mendoza—and later by Juan Boscán—is *tercetos,* which Italians were using to reproduce in the vernacular Horace's dactylic hexameters. Garcilaso de la Vega, who wrote in 1534 the first verse epistle in Spanish, used *verso suelto,* but Mendoza and Boscán, who wrote their pieces around 1539, preferred the Italian tradition. Mendoza's subject matter in *Epístolas* 2–4 and 7 is definitely moralistic, setting the precedent for a strong emphasis on the Aristotelian Golden Mean and the Senecan *Ataraxia* seen in all later specimens of the genre. As D. J. Palmer noted of Horace in a perceptive study of the English verse epistle: "His own description of his epistles as *sermones,* or 'conversations,' was appropriate to their familiar style, and their main themes—the praise of retiredness and the discussion of literature—became the principal subjects of the sixteenth- and seventeenth-century epistle. Yet Horace was not the only begetter; the poets followed a general prescription of epistolary form inherited from the classical tradition, in which Seneca's moral epistles were of almost equal importance."[35] Palmer forthwith accumulates a substantial list of characteristic motifs in the Renaissance verse epistle: "virtue and the moral life," "stoical advice," "the stoic emphasis upon living to oneself," "the Horatian discussion of motives to virtue ('oderunt peccare boni virtutis amore')," "the Horatian ideal of equanimity," "stoic sententiousness," "the stoical emphasis upon self-knowledge." In summary: "The theme of these epistles, 'seeke wee then our selves in our selves,' is appropriate to a form which was conceived to be a true image of the writer's mind, for the stoic virtues of self-knowledge and integrity are entailed by the epistle's evaluation of personal experience. In the sense that empiricism has to do with knowledge tested and authenticated in experience, it is closely related to stoicism in the epistle by a common emphasis upon the authority of the self."[36]

The epistle by Mendoza that most closely adheres to this general
description is his famous *Epístola* 2: "A Boscán."[37] Its first one hundred verses are based on the opening thirty-five lines of Horace's sixth
epistle (book 1), "Nil Admirari." The four initial strophes of don
Diego's poem, beautiful in their own right, translate faithfully Horace's first six lines:

> El no maravillarse hombre de nada,
> me parece, Boscán, ser una cosa
> que basta a darnos vida descansada.
>   Esta orden del cielo presurosa,
> este tiempo que huye por momentos,
> las estrellas y el sol que no reposa,
>   hombres hay que lo miran muy exentos,
> y el miedo no les trae falsas visiones
> ni piensan en extraños movimientos.
>   ¡Qué juzgas de la tierra y sus rincones,
> del espacioso mar, que así enriquece
> los apartados Indios con sus dones?
>
>   (*OP,* 106)

To not marvel at anything seems to me, Boscán, to be a thing sufficient to
give us a carefree life. This swift order of the heavens, the time that flees
from us by seconds, the stars, and the sun that never rests, such are those
who look at it exempt from all care, and fear does not bring them false vi-
sions nor do they think about contrary movements. What do you think of
the earth and its corners, of the spacious sea, that the faraway Indians enrich
with their gifts?

Don Diego then adds twelve lines of his own on the vanity and
haughtiness of courtiers and favorites, to return to Horace for inspiration in the next eighteen lines:[39]

> El que teme y desea están sujetos
> a una misma mudanza, a un sentimiento;
> de entrambos son los actos imperfetos.
>   Entrambos sienten un remordimiento,
> maravíllanse entrambos de que quiera;
> a entrambos turba un miedo el pensamiento.
>   Si se duele, si huelga o ya si espera,
> si teme, todo es uno, pues están
> a esperar mal o bien de una manera.

En cualquier novedad que se verán,
sea menos o más que su esperanza,
con el ánimo clavados estarán.
El cuerpo y ojos sin hacer mudanza,
con las manos adelante por tomar
o excusar lo que huye o no se alcanza.
El sabio se podrá loco llamar,
y el justo injusto, el día que forzase
a pasar la virtud de su lugar.

(*OP,* 107)

He who fears and he who hopes, both are subject to the same changes of fortune, the same sentiments; the acts of both are imperfect. Both feel the same remorse, both marvel with the same desires, one fear disturbs the thoughts of both. If one suffers, if he doubts or if he hopes, if he fears, all is one, since they are expecting good or bad in the same way. For any kind of novelty that they encounter, be it less or more than their hope, they will be with elevated spirits; without moving their body and eyes, with their hands forward to take or make excuses for what flees or what cannot be achieved. Even the wise man should be called crazy, the just man unjust, the day that virtue should force him to move from his proper place.

After this Horatian introduction, Mendoza sets out on his own to develop the theme of the *Aurea Mediocritas.* He speaks again directly to Boscán, who admires riches, beauty, honor, glory, and popularity, and who works long hours for them, concluding with the moral:

El hombre justo y bueno no es movido
por ninguna destreza de ejercicios,
por oro ni metal bien esculpido.
No por las pesadumbres de edificios,
adonde la grandeza vence al arte,
y es natura sacada de sus quicios.
No por el que procura vana parte,
y con el ojo gobernar el mundo,
forzando a la fortuna, aunque se aparte.
No por la pena eterna del profundo,
no por la vida larga o presta muerte,
no por ser uno solo y sin segundo.
Siempre vive contento con su suerte,
buena o mediana, como él se la hace,
y nunca estará más ni menos fuerte.

Cualquier tiempo que llegue, aquel le place,
cuando no puede huir la triste vez,
y búrlase de aquel a quien desplace.
   Todo se mide, de sí mismo es juez,
reposado en su vida está y seguro,
uno en la juventud y en la vejez.
   Es por de dentro y por de fuera puro,
piensa en sí lo que dice y lo que ha hecho,
duro en creer, y en esperar más duro.
   En cualquier medio vive satisfecho,
procura de ordenar, en cuanto puede,
que en todo la razón venza al provecho.
                                        (*OP,* 109–10)

The good and just man is not moved by any dexterity in drills; nor by gold
or sculpted metal; nor by the weight of buildings where grandeur conquers
art; for it is nature out of order; nor by he who attempts vainly to govern
the world, forcing dame Fortune's hand even when she flees from him; nor
by the eternal pain of Hell; nor by long life or sudden death; nor by being
first, without a second. He always lives content with his fate, good or aver-
age, as it comes to him, for he will never be more or less strong. Whatever
time that may come pleases him, if he cannot flee sad times, and he laughs
at him who is displeased at things. All is measured, he is judge of himself,
he is restful and secure with his life, either in youth or old age. He is pure
inside and out. He ponders what he says and what he has done, strong in
fear and stronger in hope. He lives satisfied with any mean, he procures to
order all that he can, for in all Reason conquers profit.

Mendoza qualifies this by reminding Boscán that the above does not
mean a man should totally reject everything; quite the contrary, he
should strive for a softness and a gentleness in all he does, blending
the two extremes ("mezclando de lo dulce con lo amargo, / y el de-
leite con la severidad"). Finally, he turns to his own state in life and
remarks:

La noche del olvido me cubriese
en esta medianía comedida,
y el vano vulgo no me conociese.
   Entonces haría yo sabrosa vida,
libre de las mareas del gobierno
y de loca esperanza desabrida.
                                        (*OP,* 111–12)

May the forgetfulness of night cover me in this restrained Golden Mean, and may the vain masses not recognize me. Then I would have a delightful life, free from the tidal changes of government and crazy hopes.

This section leads to twenty lines of "alabanza de aldea y meno-sprecio de corte," which breathe a true flavor of the good country life. Mendoza invites Boscán and his friends Jerónimo Agustín, Mosén Durall, Monleón, and Gutierre de Cetina to join him there; and here is where the normal Horatian epistle, such as Boscán's to Mendoza and Garcilaso's to Boscán, should end. But Mendoza adds to his epis-tle sixty more verses constituting a typical courtly love complaint to his lady Marfira, thereby contradicting in tone and style the very Stoic philosophy he just advocated. In fact, the only ethical statement to appear is in the last two strophes,[40] where it stands in stark contrast to the foregoing love complaint. As Elias L. Rivers has noted, "Men-doza addresses 27 lines directly to 'Marfira' in a typically Petrarchan apostrophe; though this parenthetical passage has certain pastoral ele-ments in common with its setting, it shatters the epistolary tone of the poem by its explicit exclusion of the addressee and is completely alien to the Stoic spirit of the epistle's ostensible theme of 'Nil admirari.' "[41]

Mendoza's *Epístola* 3, "A don Luis de Avila y Zúñiga,"[42] has the same meter *(tercetos),* colloquial diction, epistolary framework, and moralistic subject matter as does the poem to Boscán. Oddly, this particular poem has been unexamined by past scholars,[43] although it has at least two obvious borrowings from the classics. Malcolm C. Batchelor, who dates the poem sometime in the autumn of 1539, has noted that the tremendous description of a storm at sea ("Mira cómo nos muestra las memorias / . . . / los despojos de Persia remojados") is taken from Virgil's *Aeneid* (bk. 1, vv. 103–23).[44] The poem also contains the famous tale about Seneca's servant Hasparte, who awoke blind one day and wondered why the lights were out and the city was in darkness ("Con la mujer de Séneca vivía / . . . / decía estar a es-curas la ciudad").

Mendoza's *Epístola* 3 is perhaps his most balanced epistle. In the first thirty strophes, he presents two opposing kinds of people who make their way through life, which he follows with three strophes of comment and advice. The middle part of seventeen strophes, based on the above-mentioned passage from the *Aeneid,* presents a metaphorical description of life as a fierce storm, in which even Alexander would

throw up his hands in resignation to the gods' will. The last twenty-
one strophes are a description of how Mendoza would like to lead the
perfect life.

"How many people are there," don Diego asks his friend in the
first line, "who, making a sumptuous foundation on top of nothing,
think their good fortune has arrived." They are like little children in
the crib who have no other worry than counting the beams in the
ceiling. They go through life without any cares, and the future means
as little to them as the past did. Even changes in fortune affect them
little, for they are content with eating, sleeping, taking a *paseo*, and
thinking no one is second to them. They could not care less what is
going on in the world. They are like Hasparte, a woman who served
Seneca's wife. She awoke blind one morning and complained endlessly
about the absence of lights in the house and the dark streets. This
type of people are neither good nor bad; they are simply blind to what
is going on around them: "Este género de hombres, ni aprovecha / a
sí ni a otro, ni es malo ni bueno, / ni mira, ni provee, ni sospecha"
(*OP*, 118).

Don Diego now turns to the opposite kind of person, the one who
worries about everything. These people ponder all that has passed and
that may occur. They take the occasion when it comes, and even
search out the occasion when it is tardy. They use diligence and reason in everything, and study the world anatomically. They are always
prepared for the worst, and they take the most difficult path in every
enterprise. They literally grasp Occasion by the forelock, whether he
be awake or asleep, and drag him wherever they desire. Mendoza,
however, wants nothing to do with either of these types of people:

> En los tales que he dicho no hay remedio,
> que lo uno y lo otro me parece
> dos estremos que están lejos del medio.
>   Tomemos el camino que se ofrece,
> ni maderos espesos sin sentido,
> ni fuego que en la llama desvanece.
>   (*OP*, 119)

For those I have described there is no remedy, for each one of them seems to
me at the two extremes that are so far from the mean. Let's take the road
that is offered, neither dense numbskulls without feeling, nor a fire that dis-
sipates in the flame.

A fierce storm struck the Greek fleet, and the captains could not decide what to do. The storm scattered their ships, sunk them, drowned the mariners, and seeded the bottom of the sea with Persian riches.

> Pues viéndose crecer inconvenientes
> aquel gran Alejandro, que ganó
> eterna fama y nombre entre las gentes,
> al cielo y a los hados se rindió,
> no queriendo por fuerza procurar
> lo que Dios de su grado le quitó.
> Otro mundo es el mío, otro lugar,
> otro tiempo en que busco la ocasión
> de venirme a mi casa a descansar.
> Yo viviré la vida sin pasión,
> fuera de desconcierto y turbulencia,
> sirviendo al Rey por mi satisfacción.
> Si conmigo se extiende su clemencia,
> dándome con que viva en medianeza,
> holgaréme, y si no, terné paciencia.
>
> (*OP*, 121)

Seeing the difficulties increase, that great Alexander, who won eternal fame and renown among all peoples, surrendered to Heaven and the fates, not wishing to achieve by force what God willingly took from him. Another world is mine, another place, another time the one I look for, and the opportunity to come home to rest. I will live my life without passion, away from discontent and turbulence, serving the King satisfactorily. If he extends his clemency to me, giving me enough to live in moderation, I will be gratified, and if not, I will be patient.

There follows a description of the country life that don Diego would like to live, very similar to the "alabanza de aldea y menosprecio de corte" that Mendoza evoked in his epistle to Boscán. The presence of Marfira is fortunately played down, however; and she is depicted in a wifely role, taking quiet walks with her paramour, helping him gather apples and grapes, and watching him lend a hand to the shepherds and farmers with their rustic labors. Mendoza ends his epistle with twelve lines of brilliant self-analysis:

> A todos está bien hacer su oficio
> y gastar do quisieren su hacienda,

si viven como deben y sin vicio.
　Yo, señor don Luis, tendré la rienda,
y aun de comer, tambien como pudiere,
habido con limpieza y sin contienda.
　Si no, contentarme ha lo que tuviere,
y no me meteré a partir el cielo
con el que compañero no sufriere.
　Arrojaré mis libros por el suelo,
abriré o cerraré aquel que me place,
y andaré salpicando como suelo,
por la vía que más me satisface.

(OP, 123)

It is good that all do their jobs well and spend their income however they please, if they live as they ought and without vice. I, don Luis, will hold the reins, and even in eating also, as well as I can, with cleanliness and without conflict. If not, I will be content with what I may have, and I will not attempt to share heaven with he who accepts no partners. I will throw my books on the floor; I will open or close whichever may please me; and I will go picking and choosing as I am accustomed to, along the way that most satisfies me.

Here indeed is a happy man. It is the same philosophy as that in the epistle to Boscán, but without the unrequited love and with less emphasis on the conscious striving for virtue. The closest parallel is Fray Luis de Leon's "Vida retirada," which incorporates a number of the same themes, although the female companion is absent and distinct religious overtones replace Mendoza's clearly political background.

The Poetry of neo-Latin Inspiration

　Mendoza also received a strong "classical" influence from contemporary neo-Latin authors. In fact, a characteristic of his borrowings— as well as those of others who wrote in the vernacular—was that they were taken indiscriminately from Latin writers, regardless of the epoch. Alciati, Marullo, Calcagnini, Poliziano, and their contemporaries were treated in regard to poetic inspiration with the same respect as were the true classics. Mendoza imitated these scholars (who were likewise imitating classical models) in a number of sonnets and epigrams. Two of his most famous sonnets, "De Saladino" and "De Aníbal," derive from epigrams in Michele Marullo's *Epigrammata et*

Hymni (Florence, 1497). The first is a reflective poem on the false glories of this life and a criticism of court flatterers:

> Domado ya el Oriente, Saladino
> desplegando las bárbaras banderas
> por la orilla del Nilo, le convino
> asentar su real en la riberas.
> Lenguas le rodeaban lisonjeras,
> compañía que a los reyes de contino
> sola sigue en las burlas y en las veras,
> loándoles el bueno y mal camino.
> Contábanle el Egipto sojuzgado,
> Francia rota y el mar Rojo en cadena;
> mostrábanle su ejército y poder.
> Respondióles: —De aquí se puede ver
> donde acabó su gloria, en esta arena,
> el gran Pompeo, muerto y no enterrado.
>
> (*OP*, 13)

Having conquered the East, Saladin, unfolding his barbaric banners along the banks of the Nile, decided to establish his camp on its shore. Flattering tongues surrounded him, the only company that follows kings continually in the serious and the comic, praising the good and the bad way. They told him of subjugated Egypt, defeated France, and the Red Sea in chains; they showed him his army and power. He responded: From here one can also see where on this very beach the great Pompey ended his glory, dead and unburied.

Although Mendoza's poem follows the original quite closely,[45] it nevertheless has exceptional poetic merit. There is good alliteration ("bárbaras banderas," "lenguas . . . lisonjeras," "sola sigue") and fine use of preliminary pairs ("en las burlas y en las veras," "el bueno y mal camino," "Francia rota y el mar Rojo en cadena," "ejército y poder") which lead to the final undeceiving pair "muerto y no enterrado," a nice conceit that equates a positive and a negative and neatly refutes all that has gone before in the sonnet.

The other poem taken from Marullo is somberly meditative and exalts a famous "outsider" from the past:

> ¿Qué cuerpo yace en esta sepultura?
> ¿Quién eres tú, que encima estás sentada

mesando tus cabellos, la figura
sangrienta, de tus uñas tan rasgada?
  Los huesos y ceniza consagrada
de Aníbal, que ha pagado a la natura
la deuda postrimera, y yo la armada
diosa que en las batallas da ventura.
  Quéjome de los hados inhumanos
que a tal varón hicieron tanto mal,
y del miedo y vileza de Cartago;
  Mas quédame un consuelo en lo que hago;
que él mismo se mató, porque a Aníbal
no pudieran vencer sino sus manos.[46]

                                    (*OP*, 14)

What body lies in this sepulchre? Who are you, seated upon it tearing your
hair, your face bloody from the scratches of your nails? The bones and conse-
crated ashes of Hannibal, who has paid the last debt to nature, and I the
armed goddess that gives luck in battles. I wail against the inhuman fates
who did so much harm to such a mind, and against the fear and despicable-
ness of Carthage; but one consolation in what I do remains; that he killed
himself, because only his own hands could have ever conquered Hannibal.

Finally, Mendoza transcribed the following poem from Andrea Alciati's *Emblemata* (Augsburg, 1531):[47]

En cierto hospedaje do posaba
Amor, vino a posar también la Muerte;
o fuese por descuido o mala suerte,
al madrugar Amor, como lo usaba,
  toma de Muerte el arco y el aljaba:
(y no es mucho, si es ciego, que no acierte):
Muerte recuerda al fin, tampoco advierte
que eran de Amor las armas que llevaba.
  Sucedió deste error, que Amor pensando
enamorar mancebos libertados,
y Muerte enterrar viejos, procurando,
  vemos morir los mozos malogrados,
y los molestos viejos, que arrastrando
se van tras el vivir, enamorados.[48]

                                    (*OP*, 26–27)

At a certain inn where Love resided, Death also came to stay. Either from
carelessness or bad luck, when Love awoke he picks up Death's bow and ar-

rows (it's no surprise that he makes this mistake, since he is blind). Death finally awakes and does not notice that the arms he carries are those of Love. The result of this error was that, with Love intending to charm the young and with death trying to bury the old, we see the unfortunate young people die and the bothersome codgers dragging themselves along enamored of living.

Another epigram that is an imitation of a contemporary piece by a neo-Latin poet is Mendoza's octave entitled "De Agripina," which appears to be of classical inspiration but is also an imitation of a contemporary Latin epigram. It was not in the 1610 edition, but is, according to Knapp, most certainly by Mendoza:

> La animosa Agripina ya en reposo,
> segura de la muerte que primero
> entre miedo y respeto sospechoso
> la concertó en la nao su hijo Nero,
> vió venir el cuchillo rigoroso,
> y descubriendo el vientre al marinero:
> —Este—dijo—éste hiere ¡oh cruda mano!
> porque un monstruo parió tan inhumano.
>
> (*OP*, 229)

The spirited Agrippina, now in repose, assured of the death that first from fear and suspicious respect her son Nero prepared for her on the ship, saw the rigorous knife come, and, discovering her belly to the mariner, said: Wound this here, oh cruel hand, because it gave birth to such an inhuman monster.

The source is the epigram *Neronis impietas in matrem* by Celio Calcagnini (1479–1541), a famous Ferraran humanist.[49] Mendoza's poem actually goes beyond Calcagnini's terse epigram by elaborating the first two lines of the Latin original into six, but retaining the pithy couplet that holds the kernel of the poem. The contrast between "animosa" and "reposo," "miedo" and "respeto," and the use of repetitive sounds—"animosa Agripina," "nao . . . Nero," "vió venir"— artistically lead the reader through the sestet to the progressive "descubriendo" in line 6 and the final couplet.

This particular Spanish rendition of a Latin imitation of the Greek epigrammatic tradition is of interest because Celio Calcagnini wrote an important essay on imitation entitled "Super Imitatione Commentatis," and discussed the matter in a number of letters to friends. In an epistle to Giovanni Battista Giraldi, Calcagnini described what he considered the proper attitude of a present writer to those from the past:

It is not only disgraceful but also dangerous for one old enough to be able to stand and walk to stick always to another's footsteps (*vestigiis*) and to use what Varro calls knee-splints, since they do not easily become strong who walk with another's feet, fight with another's hands, see with another's eyes, speak with another's tongue, and who finally oblivious to themselves live with another's spirit. Now of course this is fine for those who have yet to come of age, who still eat baby food, whose limbs are still bound in swaddling bands. But those who are mature and whose muscles are stronger, let them now come out of the shade, let them now leap onto the field, let them now contend with the gladiator-trainer himself whose precepts they used to receive, and let them try their strength with him and not yield, but rather press forward, putting it to the test whether they too can be commanders and by their own prowess toss down their adversary from his position.[50]

This resentful and combative sense of imitation is, according to G. W. Pigman, from whose study the quotation is taken, typical of the final stage in a series of three varieties of rhetorical imitation—following, imitation, and emulation:

Following, or nontransformative imitation, is the gathering or borrowing of phrases, sentences, passages which amounts to a transcription of the model(s) into the text. . . . A certain amount of transforming occurs by virtue of inclusion in a new context, and complete transcription without changing a word is very rare indeed. Consequently one occasionally has difficulty distinguishing following from *imitation,* in which the note of transformation is strong. In an imitation the differences between text and model are at least as pronounced as the resemblances. . . . Critical reflection on or correction of the model distinguishes *emulation* or eristic imitation from (transformative) imitation, and this criticism is often grounded in an awareness of the historical distance between present and past.[51]

It is clear that Calcagnini thought of himself as an emulator who was composing epigrams better than those of the Romans and Greeks; and the fact that the subject matter of *Neronis* was original to him supports his claim. Mendoza, on the other hand, is an imitator. He has definitely passed beyond the stage of the lowly follower; but he is not competing with his model. This is normally true with his use of Ovid, Claudian, Virgil, and the other classical and neo-Latin writers he paraphrases; although in some cases his imitation is more non-transformative than transformative. His transcription of the passage from Pindar's Olympic ode 77 is clearly a case where the poet prefers to "walk with another's feet, fight with another's hands, see with another's eyes, speak with another's tongue."

An equally clear schema of six stages is given by José Antonio Maravall:

The sense of continuity, upon whose base the myth of the classics can be effectively developed with all its strength; the current of emulation provoked by the recognized exemplarity of the classics; the awakening of the historical consciousness that permits distinguishing and comparing epochs and human groups; the sentiment of political community that, renewed beneath the influence of the ancients in the form of partriotism, involves the defense and enlightenment of one's own group; the preferences for the moderns who, throughout the long polemic, is affirmed as a fruit of the Renaissance; the confidence in personal experience and the autonomy of reason, with its open and ample criticism of the principle of authority: such are the factors which, in the crisis of the sixteenth century, upon the base of the new socioeconomic conditions that the growth of the bourgeoisie brings with it, develop and join together to give origin to the theory of progress as a general vision of history's course.[52]

Mendoza is somewhere around stage three, "the awakening of the historical consciousness that permits distinguishing and comparing epochs and human groups," because he is clearly below the proper appraisal of his contemporaries' or his country's vernacular literature, of which he had very little in his library, depite the fact that he wrote exclusively in it.

A clearer perspective on Mendoza's place in the progress of imitative literature, as well as his attitude and role in accumulating classical artifacts, is given by Maravall in his discussion of Renaissance archeology. Maravall quotes from the *Diálogos de las medallas, inscripciones y otras antigüedades* (Tarragona, 1587) by Mendoza's close friend Antonio Agustín and notes that the author's point of view is a very different attitude from that of the enthusiasts in the first phase of humanism:

For the first humanist doctrine of imitation, the attainment of a modern version that could be confused with an ancient work is motive for the greatest admiration. For the later humanist, better equipped with historical consciousness and who, founded on it, does not pretend to confuse his time with that of the ancients, the admiration for products that the culture of the ancients has bequeathed us maintains itself only as long as they are authentic. . . . Similarly, the investigator and collector do not pretend to restore the ancients. They are modern men who study the past from their time-frame, consciously installed in the ancient world, a situation in which a self-estimation can be easily derived.[53]

Viewed from this angle of historical consciousness, don Diego clearly belongs to the second group of historically conscious collectors rather than the transcriber or copier of ancient art, while Calcagnini belongs to the earlier, more intellectually primitive group that tries to confuse its art with ancient forms. Neither belongs to Maravall's third and final group of historically conscious individuals who prefer their own vernacular art, whether past or contemporary, to Greek and Roman modes. In the literary context, Maravall outlines the threefold process as follows:

If Renaissance humanism had perhaps as its primary characteristics the veneration for Latin and Greek, that same humanism will provoke interest in and, finally, exaltation of one's own language. The process is already known to us. It begins with a primary phase in attitude of pure respect for the classical languages, to postulate next a betterment of the vernacular by imitating the ancient languages, and finally to look for the norm of one's development and perfection—a perfection that before the sixteenth century ends many will consider having been reached—in the peculiar being and context of each present language, to the point of being able to place the vernacular and the work of its authors who write in it above all whom antiquity left as inheritance.[54]

In terms of imitation, historical consciousness, and language, then, don Diego is in midstream, or perhaps a little earlier. He definitely does not belong to the last group of "modernos," but he is clearly beyond the first group of followers and transcribers.

Chapter Three
Guerra de Granada
Mendoza's Philosophy of History

In the introduction to *Guerra de Granada*[1] (War of Granada), entitled "Luis Tribaldos de Toledo al lector," the editor explains why he has decided to publish Diego Hurtado de Mendoza's history:

First, the hatred of truth is well known and very old in the world; and those who tell the truth, and ever more those who write it, normally suffer contradictions and persecutions. From the comprehension of this maxim comes the fact that all the prudent and wise historians describe events that occurred before their own times or delay publishing contemporary deeds until all the people who figure in the history have died. This is the reason our don Diego decided not to publish this history in his lifetime, desiring only, with the liberality characteristic not only of him but of the whole house of Mondéjar, to leave to future generations a complete account of what *really* happened in the war of Granada ("una entera noticia de lo que realmente so obró en la guerra de Granada"); and he could achieve it well because of his astuteness and good judgment. He was uncle of the general who began the war; he was in the very kingdom and even present at much about what he writes; he prized the truth and achieved it, as anyone who compares this book with others that have come out on the subject will easily recognize. Because in none of them do we read of our own faults or errors so frankly reported, the virtues or justifications of the enemy so well painted, the events all so verisimilar; marks by which the readers can govern themselves on the credit of what they did not see. . . . Second, now that almost sixty years have passed, and not one of those who is named here is alive, the danger of the book has ceased, since none will see himself described there; and although there are illustrious descendants or relatives of them, for a very large part of the Spanish nobility fought in this war, it would be fastidiousness and even diffidence to see any defects in the ancestor as reflecting on those who live today, when none of the defects noted are capital crimes nor the kind that diminish honor or fame; because those nobles had none, nor committed any, nor would don Diego, being who he was, have forgotten his obligations to perpetuity even when they may have been committed. Because history is written for the profit and utility of future generations, teaching them and honoring them, not angering them or affronting them, even when one wishes perhaps to bloody the pen as a warning ("Porque la histora escríbese para provecho y utilidad de los venideros, enseñándolos, y honrándolos, no corriéndolos o afrentándolos, aun cuando para escarmiento quiere tal vez ensangrentarse la pluma"). (92–93)

Tribaldos thus clarifies his motives for publishing Mendoza's book and the reasons he thinks merit its publication. His ideas are for the most part typical of those held by Renaissance historians. History offers lessons from the past that can teach future generations usefully and profitably. In the words of a later contemporary: "The study of history is customarily the happy mother of Prudence, and she who gives birth to it with less sorrow. She, with the aid of an observant consideration and reflection concerning present happenings, noting the errors and destructions of past actions, knows how to prevent and mock future ones and convert dangers into successes. Without this I do not believe anyone can possess acquired Prudence nor reign with praise."[2] The study of history can do this because, according to the historian and politician Enrique Tierno Galván, to the Renaissance mentality history functions as a real experience for the reader: "History and experience are, for the man of the sixteenth and seventeenth centuries, reciprocally reversible; history is experience, experience is history."[3]

It is this notion that causes Tribaldos to publish Hurtado de Mendoza's record of past events. Since history and experience are one and the same thing, the reader can gain an experience by reading the histories of his predecessors that is similar in its psychological impact on the ego to the original one; it has the same effect on the peruser as if he had undertaken the actions himself. In speaking of history, the seventeenth-century literary critic Luis Alfonso de Carballo stated: "Histories have another advantage, for by means of them we can say we are old men, since we know what we could know if we were born in those times when the events occurred."[4] History, in effect, *is* experience. It is not merely hypothetical reliving of past deeds recorded in chronicles that the reader undergoes, rather he actually "lives" the events in his own psychological and physical self. The reader gains the experience *qua* experience, for he becomes a "viejo" who has done those same deeds about which he reads. To carry the analogy one step further, the introspective reading of history is thought to be more efficacious than the original experience, for the vicarious reader can ponder the deed and squeeze out the very essence of meaning and significance. Miguel de Cervantes writes in his *Persiles y Sigismunda:* "The lessons from books often give a more certain experience of things than that had by the very ones who witnessed them, because he who reads attentively ponders once and many times what he is reading, and with this he exceeds visual experience."[5]

To believe that such an experiential process could be valid, Tribaldos, Carballo, Cervantes, and their contemporaries must have adhered to a philosophy of history that viewed all human actions as fundamentally uniform in execution and outcome. Evidently, they believed that the attentive reader who conscientiously applied the lessons history presented to him would be accomplishing precisely the same deeds as those in the past. Accidentally, the situation was different, being in another time and place; but substantially it was the same. A representative thinker of the time, Tomás Cerdán de Tallada, thus views history as a constantly recurring, never changing series of events: "With the memory of things past and that have occurred in other times, one sees those that can happen in future times, and in the world's deeds and even we see that the matters and things that occur, for the most part, are similar to those that occurred in other times."[6] And the Jesuit Francisco Garau presents a still deeper insight into the correlation of timeless history and the validity of imitating past occurrences: "He who wishes to foresee what is to happen to him ought to study in the history books what happened in other reigns. Because in human events, although centuries pass and individuals come and go, the causes and the events are very similar or the same. The water in a river passes and continually comes and goes, but the same river remains always. The vassals and kings are not always the same people, but the kings are always those who command and the vassals those who obey; and one ought to prepare himself for what will happen in the present by heeding what happened in the past. If the causes that functioned there penetrate and concur here, how can they not produce the same effects?"[7]

Clearly, if similar causes did not produce similar effects, if all actions were fortuitous or circumstantial, then past events would have no relation to present ones. A belief in regular patterns in nature, and consequently events in nature, was thus a prerequisite to the espousal of lessons from history. Likewise, if all human deeds are always similar throughout history, then all events are equally valuable, whether they be national occurrences or local ones, ancient deeds or modern ones, noble actions or base ones.[8] In effect, there is a clear movement during the late Middle Ages and the Renaissance from the former categories to the latter.[9] José Antonio Maravall notes that by the seventeenth century the Renaissance exaltation of honorable actions and heroic deeds had given way to the virtual opposite: "In the seventeenth century a vision of history is initiated that conceives of it as the depositary of imperfections and errors that one must overcome. It shows us, says Saavedra Fajardo, 'how actions of past governments were for the emendment of the present ones'; even more, if history 'is a drama of the ages of the world,' the consequence is that 'the errors of those who were advise those who are.' "[10] And in the same chapter Maravall quotes a telling phrase from Esteban de Garibay's *Compendio historial,* written in 1571, to the effect that "it is manifestly evident that the lessons of one's own history are more profitable and pleasing to each nation than foreign history."[11]

Hurtado de Mendoza subscribes to this basic philosophy of history. He states in the first paragraph of his book that the account of the war in Granada will be profitable and fruitful for future generations ("provechoso y de fruto para los que adelante vinieren" [95]); and he closes his introductory remarks by requesting that those who would wish to take example or warning accept his unbiased report ("agradezcan, y acepten esta mi voluntad libre, y lejos de todas las cosas de odio o de amor, los que quisieren tomar ejemplo o escarmiento" [96]). Mendoza's statement that his account will teach either by example (*ejemplo*) or by warning (*escarmiento*), and that it will be profitable (*provechoso*) and fruitful (*de fruto*) for future generations, is tailored to the general statement about Renaissance history made recently by Myron P. Gilmore that "there is the conception that to the extent to which this past can be recovered it provides moral lessons for a future generation. History is philosophy teaching by example in which the past, if correctly understood, informs and instructs the present."[12]

Mendoza is also characteristic of his age in preferring his native Spanish to Latin, in choosing a contemporary matter as his subject rather than a past one, in writing about a national theme, in stressing errors made as well as great deeds, and in seeking explanations for the events that took place. In all this he is closer to Renaissance historians like Niccolo Machiavelli, Francesco Guicciardini, and his Spanish contemporary Fernando de Herrera[13] than he is to the great systematizers like Juan de Mariana, Florián de Ocampo, and Esteban de Garibay. In effect, don Diego's first statements in the *War of Granada* concern the unusually base events he will describe:

> I well know that many of the things I shall write about will appear to some too slight and trivial for history, compared to the great things found written about Spain. . . . I choose a narrower way, troublesome, sterile, and inglorious, but profitable and fruitful for future generations: lowly beginnings, bandit rebellions, slave conspiracies, village riots, envies, hatreds, ambitions and false hopes; the delay of provisions, the lack of money, unbelieved or underestimated problems; weakness and remissiveness of spirit in people accustomed to understand, to provide, and to take responsibility for greater things. And therefore it will not be a waste of time to consider how such trivial beginnings and particular causes reach a climax in great troubles, difficulties, and public harm almost beyond remedy. (96–97)

He will thus describe a local and little estimated war that eventually involved all the great military leaders of Spain, including don Juan de Austria, the son of Emperor Charles V:

> In summary, fighting every day with the enemy, cold, heat, hunger, lack of munitions and equipment for every sector, new losses, and continual deaths; until we saw the enemy, a bellicose nation, united, armed, and knowing the terrain, favored by the Berbers and the Turks, conquered, submitted, taken from their land, and dispossessed of their houses and goods, imprisoned, tied men, women, and children together, sold at auction or taken to live in lands far from their own; a captivity and transmigration no less than those of other peoples read about in history books. A doubtful victory, and concerning such dangerous events that sometimes one was in doubt if it was us or the enemy whom God wished to chastise. (96)

These statements indeed ally Mendoza's philosophy of history to those of Machiavelli, Guicciardini, and Herrera; yet they also demonstrate the extent that Mendoza has advanced beyond Renaissance concepts of historiography into a more modern approach. For one thing, he deviates more than any other historian of the period from the cardinal rule of *Dignitas*. As expressed by Peter Burke: "A history should also deal with heroic actions; anything less was beneath the 'dignity of history,' a phrase which was much used at the time. The dignity of history, for the Renaissance writer as for Tacitus, excluded 'low' people, things, or words."[14] For another, Mendoza follows standard

Renaissance traditions by including certain set pieces that break the
action and relieve the tediousness of the account. Specifically, he presents typical "origins of cities" pieces for Granada (97–100, 220–22),
Almería (207–9), Fez, Tunis, and Algiers (236–41), and Sevilla
(370–75).

Mendoza breaks radically with the Renaissance use of the more
common set pieces that concern characters, battles, and speeches. Peter Burke devotes one chapter[15] to these three, noting that "characters, battles, and speeches tended to assume stereotyped forms, just
as painters tended to imitate classical gestures and poets to follow
classical *topoi.*"[16] This statement patently does not apply to *War of
Granada.* For yet another, Mendoza's style is quite cramped and often
unclear. Bernardo Blanco-González has called it "a model of the prose
of transition from the Renaissance to the Baroque" (64), which is ac-
curate chronologically; but Julio Caro Baroja is closer to the truth in
describing it as "voluntarily obscure and reticent," "choppy and sen-
tentious."[17] By anyone's standards, the style of the *War of Granada*
definitely does not comply with the general statement of Peter Burke
that during the Renaissance, history was often thought of as a branch
of rhetoric. Form was sometimes thought of as more important than
content; a good style more important than an interest in what had
actually happened and why. By the same token, Mendoza intention-
ally breaks the cardinal Renaissance rule of Beauty adopted from the
Platonists. The following description of rhetorical practice by Peter
Burke definitely does *not* apply to don Diego's book: "What mattered
to the Renaissance historian was not to convey any precise indication
of the individuality of *this* man, or to describe precisely what was said
or done on *this* occasion, but to give a general impression of *a* leader,
a battle, *an* oration. If the evidence was not available, it was permissi-
ble—here is the rub—to invent."[18] Mendoza's adherence to truth and
veracity is of course the exact opposite of this, as will be seen in this
chapter.

Mendoza's style is unquestionably his own. If it is based on any
technique or genre, it is the diplomatic report, much like the hundreds that he wrote for the emperor from Italy when he was the imperial ambassador. The precision, the choppy sentences that penetrate
directly to the heart of the matter, the endless enumeration of facts,
dates, and numbers, all are characteristic of an official report. The absence of chapter divisions of any kind in the early manuscripts sub-
stantiates this. Tribaldos, however, evidently wanted the work to

look like a typical history; so he broke the text into four "books" of equal length. The text clearly does not justify these divisions, since they all occur in the middle of ongoing skirmishes or campaigns. Nevertheless, the analysis of the *War of Granada* that follows will respect the divisions for their convenience in portioning the length of the text. It will also follow the progress of events precisely as Mendoza describes them, adding only dates and biographical data to better orient the reader.

Book 1

Aware that he is writing a historical document rather than a literary piece and that causes are often as important as outcomes, don Diego begins *ab initio,* with the early days of Granada when it was taken under the Spanish aegis by Ferdinand and Isabel. The city agreed to surrender in the fall of 1491, and on 2 January 1492 the Christians entered and established their government in the Alhambra. The terms for the surrender of the city were very lenient. The Moors were allowed to possess their lands in perpetuity, to be protected from all oppression, to practice their habits and customs, to worship as they pleased, to have their own courts of Arab law, to pay no more taxes than they paid under the native kings, to have their own schools, and to come and go in the kingdom without impediment.[19]

The Catholic monarchs named don Iñigo López de Mendoza, second count of Tendilla (and after 1512 Marqués de Mondéjar), the captain-general of the city, and they named the Jeronimite friar Fernando de Toledo the prelate of Granada. During the first eight years of Christian occupation the situation remained quite stable, mainly because Iñigo López de Mendoza (don Diego's father)[20] upheld the liberal terms of the pact signed by the Spanish monarchs and the Moors. The attitude of Ferdinand and Isabel was so magnanimous, in fact, that in 1497, when King Manoel of Portugal expelled all the Moors from his country, the Spanish monarchs granted them unrestricted rights to settle and start a new life in Spain.

Eventually the attitudes of the administrative officers began to change. In 1499, Granada was put under the auspices of the Inquisition of Córdoba, whose administrator was the infamous Diego Rodríguez Lucero. This same year, the Spanish kings paid an official visit to Granada (July to November). Dissatisfied with Hernando de Talavera's efforts at converting the Moors to Christianity, they decided to bring in Francisco Ximénez de Cisneros, the archbishop of Toledo. Cisneros placed so many religious sanctions and hardships on the population that in March 1500 the Moors of the Albaicín—the Arab neighborhood of the now Christian city of Granada—rebelled and set up forty "electors" to govern them. The count of Tendilla entered the Albaicín under a white flag and wrote up an agreement with the inhabitants promising not to bother any Christian Moors (who would from thenceforth be called Moriscos), to let them continue to wear Moorish garments and to speak Arabic, and to exempt them from the Inquisition. Nevertheless, the rebellion spread to the outlying villages of Güejar, Lanjarón, Andarax, and the Sierra Bermeja. This alarmed Ferdinand and Isabel, and they raised an army as large as the one for the conquest itself and marched back into Granada. The troops, under the command of Tendilla, forced the village people back into submission, massacring the inhabitants of Güejar ("pasando a cuchillo los moradores y defensores" [102]). The Spanish government then undertook the first of many expulsions, declaring on 12 February 1502 that all Moors who refused to convert to Christianity would have to leave the country. From thenceforth there would be no more Spanish Arabs, but only Arab Christians.

After these events the country was at peace for a number of years, mainly because the native inhabitants took part in political affairs and the Mendoza family was lenient and friendly with them. But, in don Diego's words, "esto se acabó con la vida de los viejos" (104). In the 1550s, with the death of the emperor and the ascendancy of Philip II, a new breed of administrators began to rule Spain and the city of Granada. Jealousies between the Granadan civil authorities, represented by the Chancillery, and the military authorities, led by Luis Hurtado de Mendoza, don Diego's grandnephew, divided the region.[21] By 1566, things had come to a head. The international situation was complicated by a recent resurgence of Arab advances in the eastern Mediterranean and along the Barbary coast. The Turks had reconquered Tripoli in 1551, El Peñón de Vélez de la Gómera in 1554, and Bougie in 1555. When Philip II took the throne, the only Spanish possessions in Africa were Melilla, Orán, Mazalquivir, and La Goleta, the fort guarding the harbor at Tunis which Charles V had taken in 1535. Philip immediately ran into trouble. In 1556 the Turks took Tripoli from the Knights of St. John and there was the real danger that the Christians would lose control of the narrow pass between Africa and Sicily. Philip therefore formed in 1559 a fleet of twelve thousand soldiers in Sicily, which advanced on Djerba (Los Gelves) in the Gulf of Khaber. It took the island and set up winter quarters with the intention of attacking Tripoli in the spring. But in March the Turks under Piali Pasha surprised the Christian forces and immediately imprisoned over five thousand soldiers. Three months later the rest of the force, starving and without water, surrendered to the Turks.[22]

Within Spain, the Moriscos had continual contact with their Arab brothers. With the Turks advancing in the west and threatening Cyprus and Tunis (both of which they seized in 1570), the question of national security became a critical one for the Spanish government. The Moriscos in the south began to be looked upon as a fifth column in the Arab campaign; and, as A. C. Hess notes, there is no other way they could have been viewed: "Transcending concerns for religious purity and economic advantage, the Muslim advance in the Maghreb vigorously raised the issue of security. If Ottoman power reached the Strait of Gibraltar, how loyal would the Moriscos be?"[23]

There was thus every reason for Philip II to be preoccupied about the security of his southeastern flank. R. Trevor Davies creates a very plausible series of events that could have led to Spain's downfall:

In fighting the Moriscos of Granada it is not too much to say that the Spanish Empire was fighting for its very life. It was good fortune rather than anything else that saved it. If the Turk had exploited the situation to the full, as the Grand Vizir, Mohammed Sokolli, wanted to do, the rebellion in that favorable quarter might well have grown too powerful to be quelled. As luck would have it, the Turk concentrated his effort against Venice instead. Had really large forces been sent to help the rebels the revolt would probably have spread to the great Morisco population of Valencia and Catalonia, which, as things were, followed the traditions of Spanish localism in standing quite apart from the affairs of Castile. Valencia and Catalonia in arms would, possibly, have been aided by Huguenot forces from beyond the Pyrenees, and the weak hub of the Spanish Empire would have cracked under the strain.[24]

In Granada, a number of administrative changes had also taken place that aggravated the tense Morisco-Christian relationship. As Mendoza describes it, Ferdinand and Isabel had placed judicial matters in the hands of lawyers (*letrados*), who were a true middle class, belonging neither to the nobility nor the lower ranks of society, and neither to the army nor the civil administrators. But the judicial matters concerning Moriscos were slowly turned over to the civil arm, represented in Granada by the Chancillery (formed in 1505 but not given any real power until 1540), which in turn was strongly supported by the church and its Inquisition. The president of the Chancillery was Pedro de Deza (ca. 1520–1600), who had earlier been a high official of the Inquisition. As an official of the church, he was not supposed to take any part in military matters. The captain-general of Granada was don Diego's nephew Iñigo Hurtado de Mendoza, third Marqués de Mondéjar (1511–80). Don Diego refers to him in the *War of Granada* as simply "el Marqués" or "Mondéjar."

One major controversy that arose in 1566 between Deza and Mondéjár concerned the jurisdiction over the Moriscos. The Chancillery decided that policing them was a part of its own civil administrative duties, and it therefore established a kind of paid local police force (*cuadrillas*) that was supposed to arrest rebel Moriscos. The Chancillery also waived the right of the feudal lords to protect the Moriscos on their estates and declared that a church could not be used for refuge beyond three days. The result of these one-sided laws, coupled with the inefficacy of the hired *caudrillas*, was that many of the Moriscos fled to the mountains to avoid persecution, forming bandit groups, called *monfíes*, that functioned almost like guerrilla armies. Mendoza sees these small bands of guerrillas as the principal element in the forthcoming war: "Estos hombres fueron el instrumento principal de la guerra" (108). The situation was made worse by renewed efforts on the part of the Inquisition to ferret out any Moriscos who may have been backsliding into the old religion ("la Inquisición los comenzó a apretar más de lo ordinario" [108]).[25]

The fact is that Deza and Mondéjar hated each other from the beginning and used every means at their disposal to damage each other's reputation, including the *cuadrillas* and the Inquisition. One seventeenth-century historian sees this hatred as actually being the major cause for the war. Julio Caro Baroja writes: "When don Pedro de Deza came to occupy the presidency, the hostility between him and the Mendoza family was such that the author of the *History of the House of Mondéjar*[26] does not vacillate in affirming that the insurrection of the Moriscos was originated by it: 'It proceeded—these are his words—from the jealousy and competition between the captain-general and the Chancillery, whose president don Pedro Deza, in order to extend his jurisdiction and diminish the military, that until then had had the government of all the Moriscos of the kingdom, persuaded the king that he should promulgate various decrees moderating the excesses of their customs, of their dress, and of their meetings, so that it could be his and the Chancillery's responsibility to catch and punish those who contravened them.' "[27]

King Philip's response was swift and rigid. Beginning on 1 January 1567, he invoked for Granada a set of prohibitions known as the Edict of 1526, because it was drawn up then by Charles V but never implemented. The document forbade the use of Arabic in any form; it took from the Moriscos all black slaves; it forced them to wear Spanish clothes, and the women to bare their faces; it ordered their houses to have the doors open on all religious feast days; it prohibited the use of public or private baths, the singing or dancing of native songs, and the holding of Moslem weddings, festivals, or parties; finally, it held the threat of taking their children away and putting them in foster homes in Castile (108).[28]

From this time the Moriscos began to make their plans to revolt. They evidently thought that they would meet with success and be able to retake southern Spain. In the area of Granada they still represented a majority of the population. They had contact with the Turks in Constantinople and with the Arabs in the Barbary States.[29] They hoped the Moriscos in Valencia would also rebel; although, as Mendoza points out, this was an illusion either because the Valencian populace was afraid of another bitter reprisal from the authorities, like the one after the aborted uprising in 1526 in the mountains around Espadán, or because the Valencians did not believe the Granadan enterprise was serious or practical. The international situation also favored the Moriscos, for Philip II was involved in warfare on every quarter. Spain at the time was preparing for war with England, was guarding its French borders from infiltrations of Huguenots, had bad relations with the German princes, was quartering a large number of troops in occupied Italy, was hindered by continual rebellions in Flanders, and, most significantly, had no troops at all within the country itself. The Moriscos, aware of the political and military climate inside and outside of Spain, began to take the first major steps to rebellion. On 27 September 1568 they met in the Albaicín of Granada and named Fernando de Válor el Zaguer, known also as Aben Xahuar, as their leader. He in turn convinced them to name his nephew Fernando de Válor as king, with the name Aben Humeya.

The first major skirmish took place on 23 December 1568, in Cadiar, where Aben Xahuar el Zaguer and a small force of townspeople murdered a small party of forty soldiers and their captain. They then marched the next night on Granada. Joining with Farax Aben Farax, they entered the Albaicín, hoping to rouse the urban Moriscos to rebellion. They met with absolutely no resistance because, oddly, there was only one small contingent of troops quartered at the Alhambra under Luis Hurtado de Mendoza (Mondéjar's son and don Diego's grandnephew, referred to throughout the book as simply Tendilla). Even more strangely, the Granadan Moriscos ignored the call to rebellion. Evidently, according to Mendoza, the Granadans knew that an uprising was about to take place, but they were not sure of the date, nor were they convinced that the call to arms on that night was the legitimate one. Moreover, the Marqués de Mondéjar, who was in charge of the troops on the walls, had learned that the Moriscos living outside the city were awaiting the sound of cannon fire as the signal to rise up in arms; so he ordered his men to stand at arms but not to fire any shots. The frustrated rebels sacked a couple of stores, burned down one of the city gates, and fled to the mountains.[30]

The next day the Marqués de Mondéjar began to put together a force of troops to pursue the marauders. By 3 January 1569 he had formed a small army consisting of his own soldiers, the *cuadrillas*, and *consegiles* (militiamen raised by the towns in the area). Within ten days, Mondéjar was at Juviles, where the first massacre of Moriscos took place. In Mendoza's words: "It happened that an undisciplined soldier began to search a woman to see if she was hiding money, and one of the Moriscos (either the husband or a relative) went to defend her, which caused such a disturbance that almost none of the Morisco men remained alive and many of the women died; some of our men were wounded because in the darkness they attacked each other" (157). The Moriscos, for their part, had started an indiscriminate slaughter of Christians on Christmas Eve, and Mendoza clearly shows a bias against their actions. He describes how the Moriscos of the Alpujarra began to desecrate and burn the churches and to massacre the priests and old Christians in the area. In Guecija some Augustinian friars hid in the bell tower, only to have the Moriscos dump boiling oil on them. They filled the priest of Mairena with gun powder and blew him up, and they buried the vicar to the waist and used him as a target for their short lances. Some they handed over to the women to be killed with sewing needles; others were stoned to death, and a few, like the children of Arze and the mayor of La Peza, were crucified. Mendoza then adds: "It was a grand testimony to our faith, and can be compared to the age of the Apostles, where among such a large number of people who died at the hands of infidels there was not one who wished to recant (although all or most of them were persuaded and tempted with safety, authority, and riches, and threats and examples of punishment); on the contrary, with humility and Christian patience the mothers comforted their children, the children their mothers, the priests their congregation, and many offered themselves willingly to martyrdom" (141–42). Mendoza adds that most of these persecutions took place in the heat of the first days of rebellion, and that Aben Xahuar and others tried to stop them by passing a law that prohibited the murder of children under ten and defenseless men and women.

Book 2

The division between books 1 and 2 is arbitrary, since it splits the expedition of the Marqués de Mondéjar in half. Apart from a brief mention of the presence in the campaign of Luis Fajardo, Marqués de Vélez (also referred to as simply "el Marqués"),[31] who set out the first week in January from Almería at the request of Pedro de Deza and in direct defiance of Mondéjar's wishes, the entire first section of book 2 concerns Mondéjar's expedition. It is not all laudatory. In fact, there are times when the reader feels that don Diego is writing antihistory about antiheroes and the mistakes they make. The only skirmish he describes by Vélez, for example, is terse and uncomplimentary: "The first campaign was against a large band of Moors who lawlessly crossed into Illar, near Féliz. Vélez took it and sacked it, enriching his people. The battle was risky and hard fought; many of the enemy died, *but more women than men*" (165–66).

Another example of how the author tends to stress the antiheroism and folly of the war is in his description of the actions of Juan de Villarroel, son of the governor of Cazorla and nephew of the already-mentioned Cardinal Francisco Ximénez de Cisneros. Don Juan de Villarroel was captain of Almería. He had seen some action with Moors before; but, in Mendoza's words, "he had become popular by finding faults in Captain-Generals, being at times listened to and even remunerated" (171). This don Juan stayed up all night convincing Mondéjar that he should be allowed to scout the Morisco encampment on

the hilltop at Las Guájaras. Mondéjar finally let him take fifty soldiers
to reconnoitre the bottom of the hill, but not to ascend into the Morisco camps.

But don Juan began to scale the slope without stopping, even though the
Marqués called out to him; and many important people and other disobedi-
ent soldiers followed him, either to show their bravery or out of greed for
loot. Over eight hundred were climbing before the Marqués could stop
them, because don Juan, seeing the number of soldiers increase and having
greater hopes for victory, thinking himself the man of the hour, without
keeping any order, . . . began to climb with the impetus and haste of one
who has no idea of what could occur; but after a while he became weak and
tired. When the enemy saw the disorder, they made a show of hiding behind
the hill to make it look like they wanted to escape. Our troops believed it
and hastened up the hill. Their tiredness increased and they lost any sense of
order. . . . They were only halfway to the top when they began to pass their
arms up. The enemy heard this and, seeing the disorder, about forty under
Al Zamar jumped out. They had few guns and did not look like soldiers;
but with the terrain in their favor, and armed with rocks that they threw
from the hill down the slope, and with a few more who came to fight with
them, they gave our soldiers such a heavy volley that they all turned their
backs and fled quicker than they had gone up without one soldier even at-
tempting to fight. The captains followed, trying to stop the men from fleeing. The Moors' numbers increased and they kept killing the soldiers all the
way down to the riverbank. Don Juan de Villarroel died completely ex-
hausted with his sword still in its scabbard, stabbed in the head and the
hands. . . . There were more dead than there were Moors who attacked
them, and some died from exhaustion. (172–73)

The next day the rear guard arrived and Mondéjar attacked Las Guájaras in force. "By order of the Marqués, no one was pardoned, regardless of sex or age; the looting was great and the deaths were
greater, especially of women" (175).

There is certainly nothing heroic or even valiant about this episode.
Mendoza describes it in the evenest terms possible, but it is clear that
he condemns rash acts like those of Juan de Villarroel. After his own
long years of campaigning in Italy, he must have viewed with horror
the looting and senseless murdering that went on every time the
Christians siezed a Morisco village.

With the victory at Guájar, Mondéjar considers the war over. He
returns to Orjiva and reports to Deza that the Moriscos want peace
and will accept any settlement given by the Christians. It is now

mid-February. The only other force in the field is the army under Vélez, which has also retired from the high sierra to Terque, where it will remain until mid-May.

Back in Granada, however, now that the danger appeared over, the city officials began to scheme and jockey for power again. They wrote to Madrid saying Mondéjar was inefficient, could not control his soldiers, did not supply his army properly, and neglected to give the king one fifth of the booty, as was required. Deza in particular asked that Mondéjar be replaced by Vélez as the military commander for the area. Mondéjar's friends defended his position at length (which defense Mendoza includes, 180–86). The result of the dissension was to give the Moriscos time and hope to reorganize their forces. King Philip was very well informed of all matters, because he had earlier sent two of his staff, Antonio de Luna and Juan de Mendoza, to fill positions left vacant when Mondéjar took the field. The king was also well aware of the international consequences of the war in the Alpujarras. As Mendoza points out, Philip feared in particular a mass invasion by the Berbers. He was receiving information at that same time about a large buildup of the Turkish fleet, which apparently was going to be directed at Cyprus, but which could just as easily sail for Spain. Finally, the king was evidently disturbed by the bad showing of the troops in Granada, especially in a recent skirmish near Válor where Vélez's troops were virtually annihilated (described by Mendoza, 192–95). He therefore decided in early April 1569 to withdraw Mondéjar from the field and to send his own brother don Juan de Austria to lead the Spanish troops in what would be a total destruction once and for all of the danger to Spain's eastern coastline.

The remainder of book 2 treats the deteriorating situation from this time to the arrival of don Juan de Austria in mid-May. One of the most tragic occurrences took place in late March when the people of Granada broke into a jail where one hundred and fifty Moriscos were being held under security arrest and slaughtered them all. Almost simultaneously, a Spanish force was attacked in Talera and annihilated. A counterattack was undertaken, but it went so slowly and was so disorganized that few of the enemy were killed, "and of those most were old and infirm people" (226). On 23 June don Juan de Mendoza ordered all the Moriscos in the city of Granada enclosed in the churches for immediate deportation. Many of the men fled to the mountains to join the rebels, and the rest were sent to safe areas in Andalucía and Granada. "It was an exile of great compassion for whomever had seen them happy and content in their homes. Many died on the road from overwork, fatigue, sorrow, hunger, or murder at the hands of the same who were supposed to guard them, who instead robbed and sold them into slavery" (230).

Mendoza reports that thirty-five hundred people were involved in this first exodus of Moriscos from the kingdom of Granada, although other sources place the number at a minimum of five thousand. It was only the first of a number of deportations that took place before the final decree of 1 November 1570. In December–January, two thousand more Moriscos are expelled from the city; in March 1570, five to six thousand are moved off the Vega of Granada; and in May a thousand men left Tolox, Monda, and Guaro, with the women and children following later.[32]

The result of this first displacement was to eliminate the city's food supply, which had been in the hands of the Morisco merchants and farmers. There was so little to eat that the people in the city began to show up for roll-calls of the soldiers to get food, and pilferage was commonplace. The authorities stopped taking roll-calls for the *cuadrillas* to avoid the disorder and decided to allow the thievery—especially when it concerned taking from the Moriscos in the nearby villages—for fear that otherwise the soldiers would mutiny or desert. The end result was to force the peaceful Moriscos living in the Vega, or plain around Granada, to flee into the mountains. "The Vega was on the point of rebelling, where every day individuals and whole villages went over to the enemy, giving as a reason that they could not bear the kidnapping of people, the robbing of household goods, the raping of wives and daughters, the imprisonments, and the murders" (212).

Book 3

Here again the break between books 2 and 3 is totally artificial, for the circumstances did not change until December 1569, when Juan de Austria took command of the forces in the field. Events in book 3 up to that point (242–312) continued to be disasters or hollow victories for the Spanish army. The first campaign narrated, for example, is that of Frigiliana, which, as with most earlier frontal attacks, resulted in some loss of life to the Spaniards and devastating effects on the Moriscos. The sack of the city resulted in the demise of five hundred men ("the large part, old men") and thirteen hundred women and children (246). Despite the apparent victory, Mendoza states that no less than six hundred Spaniards were lost in the battle. Of worse credit in the victory was the greed and lawlessness of the soldiers on entering the city. Mendoza condemns unconditionally the soldiers' actions:

> Selling of prisoners and partitioning the booty is customary in Spain; and a fifth of everything for the crown is an ancient right of kings from the first, don Pelayo, when paying and keeping troops was difficult. Now, because the booty is large, they split it up by recognition and seniority, or the kings grant the fifth in common and as a prize for those who fight well as a prod for high spirits, which is contrary to letting each one have what he may grab and giving the royal fifth equally to all who come to the war as a way to foment a stronger will to fight. For this last system breeds greed, and each one has for his own whatever he wins, so much that he stops fighting to protect it, from which are born great inconveniences for the ignorant and inexperienced soldiers. Some flee with the booty; others, hindered and weakened, let themselves be killed over it by the enemy; others throw down their banners and return to their homes with the loot. The armies made up of militia forces who live at home are undone in this way. In Italy the same thing happens among the native forces as has been seen in this war inside Spain. (247–48)

The next important military exercise was a burn and destroy mission through Restaval, Pinillos, Belexix, Cónchar, and Albuñuelas by twelve hundred cavalry under don Antonio de Luna. As usual, the troops became so disorganized from robbing, burning, and plundering that the Moriscos isolated and killed many of them. The result of the Spanish army's efforts was to desolate the land to the point that there was no food for them to eat. Vélez's troops stationed in Adra on the coast below Granada resorted to eating fish and nothing else: "A large camp, armed, full of civilians, that was large enough for a war against the Barbary States, began to weaken from catching and eating fresh fish. They neglected to follow the enemy after having broken their defenses, they did not take advantage of victories, and they let the Moriscos gain strength, attack, break through the passes, arm themselves, build up provisions, and extend the war at the gateway to Spain" (261). Vélez saw the difficulty of the position, but he could not leave Adra, where he had been since the first of June, until September because he could not accumulate enough food for an eight-

day march. Finally, on 9 September he made a successful trek to Lacalahorra, where he again remained inactive until November. The situation was almost as bad there, and desertion was so high that Vélez
ended up with less than half the troops with which he had begun.

The problems and inactivities of Vélez led to his being criticized
harshly by almost everyone but Pedro de Deza, the president of the
Granadan Chancillery. Don Juan de Austria, who had been in Granada since 12 April, tried to put the pieces together. Vélez, the high-
est commander in the field, seldom moved his troops into action;
when they did go on an attack their greed for plunder led to lost battles and renewed hatred among the Moriscos. Mondéjar had not been
in the field for a year, and he was finally called to Madrid (on 3 September) to remove him completely from the action. Juan de Austria
had plenty of troops, because forces came from all over Spain for the
privilege of fighting under King Philip's younger brother. Don Juan
also had the duke of Sesa available for the field; but Austria was still
taking commands directly from the king, who was reluctant to let
the twenty-two-year-old youth take the field in front of an army.

The situation came to a head in November when Vélez finally
moved his troops into the mountains to seize the town of Fiñana.
This was as badly planned as most of the other operations, and Vélez
lost more men than he conquered. Conditions would certainly have
never become better if the Spaniards had not been aided at this time
by the murder of Aben Humeya. Mendoza sees this act as the turning
point in the war, and devotes sixteen pages to the occurrence. In September, Aben Humeya had turned the tables on the Spaniards by in-
vading the feudal lands of the Marqués de Vélez in southwest Granada
and pillaging the area. He then returned to Andarax, his mountain
capital, and, in Mendoza's words, "vivía ya con estado de rey" (285).
But Aben Humeya was a tyrant and a miser. His dictatorial ways had
lost him friends and a number of his captains, and had caused the
Turkish mercenaries to complain about him to Constantinople. Aben
Humeya's best friend throughout the war was his cousin Abdalá
Abenabó de Mecina de Bombarón, also known as Diego López Aben
Aboó, who served as the commanding general of the Morisco forces
and was well liked by his troops.

Aben Humeya's death, which reads like the plot of a romantic
novel, occurred as follows: When the insurrection took place, it was
agreed that no Moriscos would be allowed to keep any woman except
their wives. But Aben Humeya decided he wanted a certain woman,

Zara, widow of the Morisco Vicente de Rojas, who was a relative of Aben Humeya's father-in-law. Zara was at the time living as the concubine of her cousin Diego Alguacil. Aben Humeya took her from him and kept her in his own house. Zara, offended because Aben Humeya already had wives and had taken her as a concubine, asked Diego Alguacil to rescue her. Humeya learned of the plan and Alguacil had to flee with some other Moriscos into the mountains. A few days later, Alguacil intercepted one of Aben Humeya's messengers with a letter intended for some Turkish troops. He killed the messenger and then had a nephew of his who once was the scribe for the illiterate Aben Humeya write another one to Abenabó ordering the Morisco general to murder all the Turks in his service (the Turks to whom the original letter was written) as well as Diego Alguacil, whom he was also sending to serve Abenabó. Alguacil sent the letter with one of his closest comrades and timed his own arrival to coincide with that of the letter. When Abenabó received the order, he did not know what to do. He showed the letter to Hhusceni, the head of the Turkish troops, and to Alguacil; and they all decided that the true remedy would be to assassinate Aben Humeya, seize his enormous treasure, and make Abenabó king of the Moriscos.

They set out for Andarax and one evening stole into Aben Humeya's palace, finding him unarmed and naked with two women, one of whom was the widow Zara. The next morning they held a trial in which they showed Aben Humeya the letter he had supposedly written and condemned him to die. The following day he was beheaded in the public square and his goods and women were distributed among the Morisco chiefs. The final irony to this novelesque episode is that Aben Humeya declared before his death that his intention had never been to convert to Islam and that he was dying as a Christian martyr. Alguacil of course got his concubine back. Later he fled to Tetuán, where legend has it that he was killed years later by the Turk Huzen over concubinage rights to the same Zara.

The death of Aben Humeya did not alter the internal structure of the Morisco kingdom. In fact, the changes were for the better, because Abenabó was a more intelligent person than Aben Humeya and had a craftier sense of guerrilla warfare. The psychological effect on the Christians was enormous, however; for with Humeya's death they believed that the opportunity had come to attack the Moriscos in full force. And the tide of the war indeed changed, for the only disaster suffered by the Christians after September was the fall of Orjiva to the Moriscos. It was the first and only city that they actually took from the Spaniards, and then because the troops inside had no provisions and decided to abandon it rather than starve to death.

It is at this point in his narrative, immediately before Juan de Austria took command of the troops, that Mendoza looks at the causes for the successive defeats of the Spaniards before a clearly inferior force:

Considering the causes why such a spirited nation, so adapted to suffer travails, so renowned for loyalty, so preoccupied about honor (for war is not a thing of little importance), should act in this one contrary to valor and bravery, I thought about the numerous disciplined and well-reputed armies in which I served, guided by the Emperor don Carlos, one of the greatest captains there ever was. . . . Now, on the contrary, I have never seen such a ragtag army, so disorganized, so poorly provided for, and with so much waste and loss of time and money. The soldiers are equal in fear, in greed, in little perserverance and no discipline. I think the causes to have been these. The war began in the times of the Marqués de Mondéjar with only hired local militia, to whom greed, robbing, and the weakness and few arms which the enemy possessed at the beginning invited them to come from their homes to the war almost without any order of captains or banners. They had their homes nearby to which they could return with their booty. They set out to war untrained, they remained untrained, and they returned untrained. These faults did not appear during the time that the Marqués de Mondéjar, a man of spirit and diligence who knew the conditions of his friends and enemies, had the soldiers right beside him at all times and everywhere. But after the enemy became grouped into forces, disgraces occurred by which our men became disarmed and they became armed. Fear spread from some to others, for as it is the most dangerous vice in war, it is the most contagious. They did not split up the booty equally; it was for each one what he could take, as long as he could guard it. They fled with it without union and without responding. They let themselves be killed clutching or burdened with the booty; and where they had no hope of getting any, either they did not go out to plunder, or while they were plundering they would return home. A mountain war, little provisions, less apparatus for getting them, sleeping on the ground, no wine, the pay in food stuffs, contact with little or no money, the hard work stopping when the greed for booty ceased, poor, hungry, impatient, they suffered, they died, or they were killed fleeing. Any of these groups chose as more advantageous that the war should last until they could get their hands on some booty. About the captains, some got tired of giving orders, reproaching, punishing, making the soldiers suffer. They gave into the same vices as the soldiers, and the camps in which they joined with them were that way. . . . My true consideration of these matters will not seem a profitless philosophy for the future, although experienced at our own cost and damage. (305–8)

Much of this evidently changed when in November Juan de Austria suspended for a time the commands of thirty-two of the forty-one captains, took personal charge of the troops, and planned a major offensive against Güejar de la Sierra, a town only fourteen miles from Granada that, because of its supposed impregnability, remained in Morisco hands. Austria was under the impression there were over six thousand rebels there; so he sent the duke of Sesa, Gonzalo Hernández de Córdoba, grandson of the *gran capitán* and an acquaintance of don Diego from the Italian campaigns in Milan and Lombardy, to begin the siege. On the twenty-third, he set out with his own troops from Granada. By all accounts, this expeditionary force, gathered to suppress a bunch of poor and desperate mountain people who refused to conform to the Castilian way of life, was the largest army ever assembled on Spain's soil. Mendoza describes the expedition to Güejar with exacting detail; and well he might, for it is the only military excursion that he personally participated in.

Austria sent the duke of Sesa along a short route over the mountain peaks while he took the long route along the river, for he hoped to catch the whole Morisco force in Güejar by cutting off their exit. Austria evidently did not know what kind of troops he had with him. The first setback was that he insisted on traveling at night to surprise the enemy, but his force became lost, since, as Mendoza notes, even the native guides had trouble finding their way at night through the mountains. The second was that Sesa arrived at Güejar twelve hours before don Juan, only to discover that the city was abandoned, "except for ten or twelve old men who had decided to die there rather than be a burden; they were seized and beheaded" (328). The Moriscos, informed of every move the Christians made, had left the city and hidden in the surrounding hills, from where they descended in guerrilla bands to harrass Sesa's and Austria's forces. Don Juan finally arrived at Güejar with his troops in surprisingly good order, saw the banners and troops within the city, and, thinking it was the enemy, ordered the cannon to be brought up; but Sesa sent word down that it was he and that he had already "routed" the Morisco forces. "We were shocked that Luis Quijada [don Juan's tutor and mentor] did not recognize our banners and squadron formation from so close, being a man versed in warfare and with good eyesight, and that the duke would report that the enemy was routed when there was no enemy. . . . The taking of Güejar had more renown far away than nearby, and more congratulations than enemy" (330). Sesa and don Juan returned that same night to Granada; but don Juan, determined to win a legitimate battle against the enemy, made immediate plans to attack the stronghold of La Galera.

Book 4

Don Juan left Granada for the battlefield on 29 December, charging Pedro de Deza with civilian matters, as due his position of president of the Chancillery, and the duke of Sesa with coordinating supplies and arms for the military. On 21 February Sesa took another army into the field, and Gabriel de Córdoba became the military chief in Granada. Mendoza notes that for some reason Gabriel de Córdoba retained a large number of troops to guard the Albaicín and the Vega around Granada, although both were by then completely empty of Moriscos (339).

By February, Don Juan de Austria was moving toward La Galera for what became the most famous battle of the war. When he had his forces surrounding the walled city (on 7 February), he mined the walls in two nearby places. The first bombs destroyed a large section of the battlements and the Moriscos rushed to defend the opening by building a barricade. An hour later don Juan ordered the detonation of the second mine, which destroyed all the men working on the wall and made an even larger gap. The soldiers poured into the city, murdering every living thing in it and burning the entire area "so it would no longer be a nest for rebels, and so the dead bodies would not cause any epidemic diseases" (345).

Sesa (referred to only as "el Duque" in this part of the text), had meanwhile worked his way through Padul and Lanjarón to Orjiva. Don Juan at the same time had taken the town of Serón, although he lost there his tutor and mentor Luis de Quijada, plus a third of his force who deserted to plunder the city. Sesa found himself low on food and water and sent the Marqués de la Favara to Lacalahorra with all the sick and wounded soldiers plus the captured goods and prisoners. This nobleman from Seville was not at all accustomed to the mountains or guerrilla warfare, and he allowed his vanguard and rearguard with the sick and wounded to become separated from the main

forces. On 16 April, the Moriscos, who had been following this mot-
ley army since it separated from Sesa, swooped down and slaughtered
over one thousand Christians, freeing seventy Moorish women and
three hundred animals, and all without losing one Morisco soldier.
Sesa was forced to change his course of action to the coast, where the
men could at least eat fish, but he was plagued by desertions and
small mutinies until he set his forces against Castell de Ferro and thus
gave them a chance to sack and pillage the Moriscos.

Juan de Austria, on the other hand, was having fairly good success
in subduing the area around Tíjola and Purchena; yet in May another
fiasco caused the war to flare up again. Austria sent don Antonio de
Luna to pacify the area around Ronda, and Luna's forces were so cruel
and merciless, especially in sacking Jubrique, that the Moriscos in the
area returned to the offensive: "The Moors, who were suspicious and
fearful, when they discovered our people, went into the mountains
with their arms, leaving behind houses, women, children, and cattle.
The soldiers (as is customary) began to rob, to burden themselves
with clothes, to make slaves of all kinds of people, wounding and
killing without any discrimination at all. When the Moors saw the
disorder, they came down out of the mountains and massacred the
soldiers, who, greedy and absorbed in the looting, abandoned the defense of themselves and their flags. This disorder continued until well
into the darkness of the night" (366).

Don Antonio de Luna pulled out of the area and returned to
Ronda, where his entire army literally dissolved away, because the
soldiers all set off for home with their loot or set up stalls to sell the
Moriscos like cattle at an auction. Don Antonio returned to report
the disaster to don Juan, and the area around Ronda, then without
any leadership, became even more disorderly because the Christian inhabitants rushed into the surrounding countryside to rob women,
children, and cattle; and the Moriscos, now totally without hope of
any favorable outcome, began to do the same thing to the Christians.
This impasse continued throughout the summer until don Juan sent
the duke of Arcos in September to put order in the region. It is this
campaign of Arcos (also referred to in the text simply as "el Duque")
that closes the military campaigns described by Mendoza. With the
success of that excursion, don Juan announced on 31 October that all
Moriscos were to be exiled from the kingdom of Granada forever and
to be repatriated in other parts of Spain. Austria, who had been in
Guadix with his troops from September to November, returned to

Granada and shortly afterward (30 November) left for Madrid, charging Pedro de Deza with the problem of relocating the Moriscos.

The last pages of Mendoza's book, relating the circumstances that
led to the assassination of Abenabó, the Morisco king, again resemble
an adventure novel. Although all the villages of Granada had been
taken from the Moriscos, and most of the inhabitants either murdered, sold into bondage, sent to exile in Africa, or transported to
other regions of Spain, Abenabó still held out in the mountains with
about four hundred men. Within the Christian camp there was a man
named Farax who was a friend of Gonzalo el Xeniz (or Lorenzo el
Xeniz, as other historians call him), the head of the now dispersed
Morisco forces and a close friend of Abenabó. Farax reported to Pedro
de Deza that he was certain Gonzalo el Xeniz would surrender himself
and his troops if offered a full pardon for his acts during the war.
Francisco Barredo, a rich Granadan merchant who had continued to
trade with the Moriscos throughout the war, was called in to act as
an intermediary; and he set off for the Alpujarra and arranged a secret
meeting with el Xeniz. The Morisco told Barredo that he would assassinate Abenabó only if the king of Spain himself signed a royal pardon for him and his troops. Amazingly, the pardon came from
Madrid in a very short time. It was translated into Arabic by Alonso
del Castillo,[33] and Barredo took it to el Xeniz on 13 March.

The Morisco carried out his promise immediately. On 15 March he
tricked Abenabó into going into a cave alone to meet him "about
things important to all" (400), and there he and his cohorts stoned
the Morisco chief to death. They put Abenabó over a horse, rode him
down to the valley to where Barredo was waiting, cut out his guts,
stuffed him with straw, set him on his horse, and marched him into
Granada to the steps of the Chancillery. There they cut off his head
and put it in a cage over the Rastro gateway with a sign that said:
"This is the head of the traitor Abenabó. No one shall remove it under pain of death." "Such was the end of this Moor, whom they had
for their king after Aben Humeya. Of the Moors who remained, some
surrendered and others escaped to the Barbary States, while the rest
fled to form guerrilla gangs, until the mountain cold and the rough
existence finished them; and the war and uprising ended. The land
remained unpopulated and destroyed. People came from all over Spain
to populate it, and they were given the Moriscos' farms with a small
annual pension. Francisco Barredo received six thousand ducats from
the king in the form of Morisco land and goods and a house on Aguila

street that belonged to a Spanish Jew thrown out of the kingdom. Afterward Barredo went to the Barbary States a number of times to ransom captives, and at a banquet there they killed him" (402–3).

The Aftermath

Mendoza wrote his book immediately after the events described, so he does not inform us of the overall result that the total dismantling of the Moorish civilizations in Granada had on the area; although he certainly witnessed the entire operation, since the exodus began on 1 November 1570 and was over by the end of December. On that day, the Moriscos were herded town by town into the churches and official buildings. It did not matter if they had fought against the Christians or were "moriscos de paz"; their age, sex, physical health, and political position made no difference. They were formed into groups of fifteen hundred each and escorted by companies of two hundred soldiers to different sections of Spain. They were allowed to take all their household goods, but many were robbed and even murdered along the way. One historian calculates that at least 20 percent of the exiles died before reaching their destination;[34] another puts the death rate at 30 percent.[35] In all, approximately forty thousand people were displaced during the nine weeks of November and December 1570. Fifty-five hundred went to the province of Sevilla, twenty-one thousand to Albacete, twelve thousand to Córdoba, and six thousand to Toledo. In the following months, another ten thousand were ferreted from the mountains in the Alpujarra and sent north. To these must be added the twenty thousand who were deported from the city of Granada in June 1569 and the Vega of Granada in March 1570.

The sum total of Moriscos who were exiled from Granada, then, adds up to a minimum of eighty thousand persons.[36] Calculations for the entire population of Granada reveal that this number is a little more than one half of the one hundred and fifty thousand Moriscos who resided in Granada in 1568. The other seventy thousand either fled to Africa, France, Italy, Portugal, or other parts of Spain on their own, remained hidden in the mountains, or were sold into slavery, or assimilated into the Christian remnant (approximately one hundred and twenty-five thousand Christians, or about 45 percent of the 1568 population of Granada), or perished during the war. The demographic effect on Spain is as follows. In 1568 there were one hundred and fifty thousand Moriscos in Granada, eighty-five thousand in Valencia, forty-eight thousand in Aragón, and thirty thousand in Castilla. By 1609, when another census was taken before the final expulsion of all Moriscos from Spain, there were one hundred and thirty-five thousand in Valencia, one hundred and fifteen thousand in Castilla, sixty-one thousand in Aragón, and eight thousand in Cataluña.[37]

The transfer of the Granadan Moriscos in 1570 clearly destroyed the economy and the traditional ways of life in Granada. The silk industry, which was considered the most prosperous in the Western world, was totally destroyed, and the small farming of perishable goods was lost. Two years of brutal warfare and the displacement of half of the region's population left Granada in a sad state of affairs from which it never recovered. While the population of two hundred and seventy-five thousand in 1568 descended to less than one hundred and seventy-five thousand in 1572, it had grown to only two hundred and fifteen thousand in 1591. A total of one hundred and thirty villages in the region were never repopulated, and so fell into dust. One reason for this was that Granada was a virtual outpost for the rest of Spain. In 1572, for example, five thousand Galicians set out from Orense to resettle the Vega of Granada. Most of them died along the way due to the length of the trip—one thousand kilometers—and the harsh terrain; and of those who arrived another half died in the Royal Hospital of Granada from diseases contracted along the way.[38] When settlers did arrive, they found the churches and houses stripped of everything of value, the bakeries, mills, and shop equipment destroyed, the fruit trees and fields gone to seed. They also discovered that although the land was free to them, the Granadan nobles and public officials had placed heavy taxes on both land use and crop yields, more burdensome in fact than those they had imposed on the Moriscos. The disillusionment of these poor people who traveled so far to settle on "free" land can easily be imagined, as well as the reason why very few new colonizers entered the area after the first influx in 1572–73.

While all this was transpiring, don Diego was writing his account of the wars. It was finished at least in 1572, because Jerónimo de Zurita, the noted author of *Los anales de la Corona de Aragón*, mentioned the book to Philip II in a letter of 23 January 1573 as something with which both he and the king were familiar.[39] This fact clearly discounts the romantic belief that Mendoza had not published his work because he feared the king's disapproval. No one knows why Mendoza never published any of his works. They were nevertheless well-known, as some thirty-four manuscript copies of *Guerra de Granada* testify.[40] Tribaldos's edition in Lisbon (1627) obviated the need for manuscripts and served as the standard text of the history for another fifteen editions, with over half of those appearing in the romantic period between 1830 and 1870, when interest in Arab Spain and the exotic Moors reached a peak.

Mendoza's work was also copied and imitated before 1627. Luis Cabrera de Córdoba used the book for his information on the war in *Felipe Segundo, Rey de España* (unpublished until 1876) as early as 1583; and Luis de Mármol Carvajal, who wrote his "eyewitness" account entitled *Historia del rebelión y castigo de los moriscos del Reino de Granada* in 1599,[41] not only had Mendoza's book beside him as a guide but most probably was prompted to write his own version in reply to what he considered Mendoza's harsh and biased history of the war.[42]

Another group of contemporary books that drew from Mendoza's account were the many tractates written shortly after 1610 to justify the final expulsion of the Moriscos from Spain, especially Jaime Bleda's *Defensio Fidei in Causa Neophytorum sive Morischorum Regni Valentiae totuisque Hispaniae* (Valencia, 1610) and his *Corónica de los moros de España* (Valencia, 1618).[43] But the most famous account of the war of Granada is the second part of the *Guerras civiles de Granada* by Ginés Pérez de Hita in 1619. Its content is discussed in the *The Moorish Novel* by María Soledad Carrasco-Urgoiti.[44] Lamentably for historical evidence, Pérez de Hita's version novelized the war of Granada sufficiently to give the impression that the rebellion was a wonderful, chivalresque adventure. It may well be to Pérez de Hita's version (as well as to Mármol Carvajal's) that Tribaldos refers in the prologue when he states that don Diego "prized the truth and achieved it, as anyone who compares this book with others that have come out on the subject will easily recognize" (92).

Hurtado de Mendoza's account is nothing if not truthfully and honestly reported; and these were the very traits which kept the book off the presses for over fifty years. Mendoza gives clear reasons for the rebellion of the Moriscos, and he explains in lucid detail how a war that should and could have lasted only two months was dragged out for over two years. The Spaniards were at fault in both instances, and in both it was individual leaders who were to blame: Deza, Vélez, Sesa, Luna, Juan de Mendoza, Arcos, and even nephew Iñigo Hurtado de Mendoza. If these leaders and the men who followed them had acted in a different way or had made different decisions the rebellion would not have occurred. Mendoza makes it clear that it did not *have* to happen; it was not a scientifically predictable event, based on some general notion of divine, natural, or human law (as some contemporary historians could have viewed it).[45] That is what really separates Mendoza's *War of Granada* from other histories of his time. It is not literature, nor systematic history, nor a justification for events, nor an apology for dubious actions; it is a real and honest diplomatic report of, in Tribaldos words, "what *really* happened in the war of Granada" (92).[46]

Chapter Four
The Attributed Works

The most exhaustive study on the many works attributed to Diego Hurtado de Mendoza is R. Foulché-Delbosc's "Les oeuvres attribuées a Mendoza," published in 1914.[1] Of the twenty-one works examined therein, most are declared by Foulché himself to have been wrongly attributed to Mendoza. The works of surest attribution are a lost translation of *Syrus,* a five-act comedy by Domenico Crispo Ramnusio (MS 2-E-5 in the Madrid Royal Library) that states on the last page "Comediam hanc vulgari traduxit lingua Didacus Hurtado Mendoza"; a Latin "Paraphrasis in totum Aristolelem" (MS F-II-6 in the Escorial Library); and a translation from the Greek of Aristotle's *Mechanics.*[2] None of these works falls within the scope of the present volume.

Four other works attributed to Mendoza that could very well be by him, although absolute proof is lacking, are *Lazarillo de Tormes,* the satirical pieces "Carta al Capitán Salazar" and "Diálogo entre Caronte y el ánima de Pedro Luis Farnesio," and the historical study "Lo de La Goleta y Túnez, año de 1535."

"Diálogo entre Caronte y el ánima de Pedro Luis Farnesio"

The "Dialogue between Charon and the Soul of Pier Luigi Farnese, Son of Pope Paul III" was first published in 1855 by Adolfo de Castro.[3] Pier Luigi Farnese (1503–47) had been given in 1545 the duchies of Parma and Piacenza by his father Pope Paul III (Alessandro Farnese, 1468–1549). Parma and Piacenza, two contiguous states strategically located between Milan and Bologna, were papal states and so the bestowal of them was illegal. Furthermore, Charles V had a personal interest in their status because the territories had been placed under his dominion after the sack of Rome in 1527. He had later magnanimously returned them to the Papal See when the imperial governor, the duke of Sforza, died in 1536 without heirs, with the stipulation that they never be traded or sold to another power. The bestowal of Parma and Piacenza thus was a direct offense against

Charles V; but the emperor was at the time an ally of the Pope, with whom he was involved in a joint effort against the rebellious German Protestants, generally called the Schmalkaldic War.

Charles's plans for Farnese's removal began in 1547 when Ferrante Gonzaga succeeded the deceased marquis of Vasto as duke of Milan. The emperor immediately began to plot Farnese's assassination, and Gonzaga wrote Charles in July to report that the murder was contracted. On 10 September, four noblemen from Parma had dinner with Farnese in his castle. During the meal they let in their troops, cut Pier Luigi to pieces, and threw him out the window into the moat. The next day Ferrante Gonzaga arrived with his Spanish troops and took possession of Piacenza in the name of Charles V.

Mendoza evidently knew nothing beforehand, since he affects surprise in a letter written to the emperor on 18 September.[4] The pope, who was in his seventies, almost died from the news, but did not respond directly to Gonzaga or the emperor. Instead he put don Diego—whom he believed implicated—under surveillance and forbade him to leave Rome.

Pope Paul's major action was to declare that Parma and Piacenza indeed belonged to the Holy See; but this move only alienated his grandson Ottavio Farnese, who in 1538 had married Margarita of Austria, the natural daughter of Charles V. Ottavio thus expected to inherit at least Parma from his murdered father. The question was never peaceably settled. When Julius III became pope in 1549, he continued his predecessor's efforts to regain the two duchies. Ottavio, meanwhile, invaded and seized Parma in 1551 at the head of some French troops loaned him by Henry II. Both Julius and Charles were alarmed by the French presence in Italy, especially under the command of the emperor's son-in-law, so they promptly beseiged Ottavio. By the spring of 1552 nothing had been achieved, however, and don Diego began to receive the blame for the poor outcome of the war.[5] A truce was finally concluded that went against the emperor, since it called for a suspension of warfare for two years, with Ottavio remaining in Parma.

Mendoza's dialogue was written in 1547, immediately after the assassination and long before Mendoza realized the whole episode and resulting war were to be blamed on him. The soul of Pier Luigi arrives at the short of the river Lethe. Since he is so mutilated ("sin pies ni manos camina, hendida la cabeza, como dicen, de oreja a oído, degollado y con dos estocadas por los pechos" [BAE, 36:1]), Charon does not recognize him. When he discovers his identity, he mocks Farnese's murder by citizens of his own kingdom and the use by Farnese of the title of duke, since Parma and Piacenza belong to the emperor, for which reason the pope had no right to give them away. Charon then relates what he has heard from people Farnese murdered, as well as from recently deceased men who had contact—both political and sexual—with him. There then follows a scathing attack on Pier Luigi Farnese in which the duke unwittingly reveals himself to have been a tyrant and oppressor of the masses. Farnese is also brought to task for converting a monastery into his personal fortified castle and for having, along with his father, a credulous faith in astrology and other divinatory arts.[6]

Pier Luigi then learns that the river he is to cross is the River of Forgetfulness, and he refuses to board the ship because he wishes to await the avenging of his murder, for he left contingency plans with his father and children. Charon disillusions him by letting him know that immediately after his death Ferrante Gonzaga entered Piacenza and was warmly welcomed by the populace. They in turn so hated their past master that when Gonzaga tried to bury him in church ground, the populace dug him up and threw him back into the moat. Furthermore, his son Ottavio has seized Parma and shows no interest in avenging his father's murder. Pope Paul will do nothing either, for he is on his deathbed. At that moment some of Farnese's former enemies appear and he hurriedly enters Charon's boat to escape them.

The dialogue ends with a speech by Charon, in which he defends the emperor and the newly established Council of Trent, denouncing Pope Paul III and his attempts to sabotage any efforts for reform. Charon sees the council as a chance for reunification of the Protestants and Catholics through reformation of the church, whose corruption forced the original protests ("La primera ocasión que movió a los alemanes a negar la obediencia a la Iglesia nació de la disolución del clero y de las maldades que en Roma se sufren y se cometen cada hora").[7] Reunification will in turn bring a new Christian crusade against the Infidels: "Por otra parte creo que mudada y reformada la Iglesia, los príncipes cristianos se unirán asimismo y darán sobre el Turco."[8]

The dialogue is thus a criticism of two things: Pier Luigi Farnese's rulership in Parma and Piacenza and the corruption of the papacy, seen especially in Pope Paul's superstitions and his political motivations, including "el concierto con franceses, con venecianos y con el

Turco" (*BAE,* 36:6), at the time all foes of the emperor. There is also in the dialogue the humanist ideal of a unified church under the emperor, and the typically Spanish ideal of a Christian holy war against the Moors. Mendoza sees the Council of Trent as being the factor to bring about the reformation; and at the first meeting in 1545, which Mendoza attended, there were indeed efforts to reconcile differences between the Protestants and Catholics, although Charles never could bring the two factions to sit at the same table, and Philip II, who took over control of the council in 1559, made no effort at reconciliation. On the contrary, he decided to win back lost souls by force of arms and doctrine. Don Diego's statements thus seem rather fantasized in view of what eventually occurred at Trent. Yet at the time he wrote them, there still persisted a ray of optimism in the establishment of the humanist ideal of world harmony.

In summary, the "Dialogue" accomplishes two things. It justifies completely the cold-blooded murder of Pier Luigi Farnese, and concomitantly Charles's active role in it and Mendoza's consent of it. The dialogue also serves to explain imperial policies, especially the scope and purpose of the Council of Trent. It was assuredly this justificatory role, and not solely a denunciatory one, that motivated Mendoza to write the dialogue.

"Carta al Capitán Salazar"

The "Letter to Captain Salazar"[9] was written in response to a book that the soldier wrote concerning the defeat of the Lutherans at Mühlberg on 24 April 1547 by the imperial forces under the command of the duke of Alba. Both the book and its author are unknown, although the historian Pedro de Salazar has been suggested. Mendoza directs himself to the author as if he were his friend and ally at court, relating how the book on the emperor's victory over the Saxons has been a best-seller, especially for the immense amount of detail and personal observations with which Salazar has enriched his account. Some slanderers have attacked the volume, however; and Mendoza intended to defend it publicly, but the book had so many detractors that he decided to remain quiet out of fear. Nevertheless, Mendoza will explain his method of defense to Salazar. First, the book must be good, because it says in the Bible that anything that makes one happy and raises the spirits is good. Since Salazar's book entertains everyone and makes them laugh, it must be good.

The only argument Mendoza cannot answer is the following: "If Salazar fought so much, how did he see so much? How, being surrounded by the enemy, could he see what his friends did? And if he was in front of everyone, how could he see what those in the rear were doing? And if he lingered to note what everyone else was doing, how could he have been first on every occasion?"[10] If the critics ask him about where or when Salazar studied the Roman authorities that are cited so often in the book, Mendoza can safely answer; for he knows Salazar never studied anywhere nor read in his life a commentary. As for those who laugh at Salazar's book because the captain acknowledged having written it in a few hours and was not a historian—Salazar should tell them to try and write a book in such a short time to see how well they do. And if they wonder why he wrote the book, since he was not a royal chronicler, he should answer that he is like the beggar who picks up the scraps from the table of others, or the fisherman who cleans out the net after the large fish have been selected by the more important people. Others complain that Salazar filled the book with unnecessary lists of banners taken and standards won, but Mendoza sees these as the spices and sugar in the stew. The only problem is that another book has come out in which the colors and sizes of the banners are completely different.

The one thing Mendoza would want to criticize is Salazar's use of Italianisms: *hostería* for *mesón*, *estrada* for *camino*, *forraje* for *paja*, *foso* for *casa* [*sic, cava?*], *lanzas* for *hombres de armas*, *emboscadas* for *celadas*, *corredores* for *adalides*, *marcha* for *camina*, *el caz* for *el vado*, *indignación* for *devoción* (*BAE*, 36:549). He urges Salazar to write in the language of his country "and not the mother tongue, but the modern one that is spoken in Granada since 1492."[11]

For the rest, Salazar's style is to be admired, since it is so close to the style of the books of chivalry like *Florisel de Niquea*, with phrases like "la razón de la razón, que tan sin razón por razón tenga" (*BAE*, 36:549). And if a man who knew as much as the bishop of Mondoñedo could write a simple book like *Menosprecio de la corte y alabanza de la aldea*, why cannot Salazar who is so simple write a complicated book like he did? Mendoza closes by assuring Salazar he does not want to offend him, but only help him defend his book; so he hopes they will remain friends.

This witty little essay, full of jokes, understatements, equivocations, and tongue-in-cheek praise, is a perfect example of Renaissance satire. The letter also points to Mendoza's theories about history and how it should be narrated, or better, how it should *not* be narrated. First, the historian should be a professional, well-read in the classics (specifically in the Roman commentaries), and practiced in the art of description. Second, the historian should relate only proven facts; he should not claim he was at a certain place if he was not, nor should he include verbatim speeches he did not hear, nor costumes and banners he did not see. Third, he should not praise leaders and warriors without due reason, since it will appear he is writing the history for that motive and not to relate true events. Fourth, the historian should write in a plain, direct style free of neologisms, chivalresque locutions, exaggerated detail, and unrelated references to classical writers which, in Mendoza's words, stand out like a fart at a tea party ("como cuando a uno se le suelta un pedo entre damas" [*BAE,* 76:548]. Mendoza practiced what he advocated, as his historial works well testify.

"Lo de La Goleta y Túnez"

The detailed account of Charles V's conquest of Tunis and the fort that protected that city's harbor is an object lesson for writers like Captain Salazar. The author is unknown, but a strong argument has been made by Erika Spivakovsky for Diego Hurtado de Mendoza.[12] Her major reasons are the following: (1) there is a work attributed to Mendoza by Conrad Gesner entitled "De Tunetana Expeditione," which is probably the title Gesner gave to a Latin version of don Diego's study;[13] (2) Diego Hurtado de Mendoza participated in the campaign, along with his brothers the Marqués de Mondéjar, don Bernardino, and don Francisco; (3) the manuscript is from the Escorial Library, where all of Mendoza's papers were taken in 1575 and summarily deposited on the shelves; (4) the very anonymity of the piece argues for Mendoza's authorship, since he was one of the very few writers of talent who preferred to remain anonymous; and (5) the internal evidence of style and content shows the author to be of the same mind as he who wrote *Guerra de Granada.*

The fifth reason for attributing "Lo de La Goleta y Túnez" to Mendoza is the most convincing. Besides the overwhelming impression that this whole piece reads exactly like *Guerra de Granada,* a number of particular similarities with the latter work stand out: it has an introductory geographic and historical description of the area; it is written in a Latinate style; the peculiar spelling of proper names is often the same as in Mendoza's epistles; the spirit of criticism with which the mistakes of the Spanish leaders are reported is typical of Mendoza, as are the objectivity of the report and the constant attention to causes for the events that transpired. Finally, there is the condemnation of the wild sacking of Tunis after its fall, which, as in Granada, turned a military victory into a slaughter of innocent people. Toward the end of the account, for example, the author seeks to explain how it was possible for Barbarossa to have escaped when he was completely surrounded by thousands of Christian troops. The author describes how the Arab chieftain fled across a waterless desert with a few lieutenants to Bona, where he had fourteen or fifteen ships. He then poses the rhetorical question of Barbarossa's escape ("El tomó la vía de Bona a do tenía catorce o quince galeras, las cuales puede alguno preguntar porqué no se le quemaron" [202]). First, he answers, it was impossible to send ships and men to Bona when the fortress at La Goleta was being seiged because all the troops were needed to prevent the Turks in the castle from escaping. Second, after having taken La Goleta all the commanders' time and energy were spent on attacking Tunis, a prize beside which Bona lost importance. Third and last, after Tunis was taken the soldiers and even the sailors broke ranks to loot Tunis and the neighboring villages, so there was no one capable of sailing to the city.[14]

In summary, the account is, in the author's words, "a brief true account of the things that he saw" ("una relación breve verdadera de las cosas que vió" [206]); and as such it belongs to the same kind of history as does *Guerra de Granada,* where Luis Tribaldos de Toledo stated that Mendoza's account was an "entera noticia de lo que realmente se obró en la guerra de Granada" (92). It will probably never be known for certain if Mendoza is indeed the author of "Lo de La Goleta y Túnez," but all the evidence points to him. The same is true for the "Carta al Capitán Salazar" and the "Diálogo entre Caronte y el ánima de Pedro Luis Farnesio." All three works are excellent examples of their respective genres, and Mendoza should be given credit for writing them as long as their authorship by another is not definitely proven.

Lazarillo de Tormes

The authorship of *Lazarillo de Tormes,*[15] on the other hand, is a hotly disputed controversy. The various nominees for authorship other than Diego Hurtado de Mendoza have been Juan de Ortega,[16]

Sebastián de Horozco,[17] Juan de Valdés,[18] Alfonso de Valdés,[19] Hernán Núñez de Toledo,[20] Lope de Rueda,[21] and Pedro de Rhúa.[22] The two proposed authors that should probably be discarded first are the Valdés brothers. Recent studies have argued convincingly that the *Lazarillo* was written in the early 1550s;[23] yet Alfonso died in 1532 and Juan in 1541. The attribution of the novel to Pedro de Rhúa, Lope de Rueda, or Hernan Nuñez has never been accepted by any large number of serious scholars. Juan de Ortega, while he cannot be discarded as a candidate, has only José de Sigüenza's statement in 1605 to support him, and the statement was made almost fifty years after the death of Ortega. Sebastián de Horozco thus remains the only serious candidate other than Mendoza; and, indeed, there is no proof that Horozco did *not* write the novel. On the contrary, Francisco Marquéz Villanueva (see note 7) has presented strong evidence supporting Horozco's authorship, although it is all very circumstantial.[24]

The problem of authorship has been aggravated by two other unknown factors; the date of composition and the first publication date. The former question has over the years been linked to the comment at the end of the *Lazarillo:* "Esto fue el mesmo año que nuestro victorioso emperador en esta insigne ciudad de Toledo entró y tuvo en ella Cortes, y se hicieron grandes regocijos."[25] The emperor held a Cortes in Toledo in 1525 and in 1538, and there are no other solid clues in the text to tie Lazarillo's statement to either one in particular. Clearly, if the author of *Lazarillo* were writing his book contemporaneous to the events described, then the date would be of maximum importance; for it would tell if the book were written in the late 1520s or in the early 1540s. Arguments of this kind invariably favor the latter date.[26] It is of course possible that the novel's historical time is totally unrelated to its date of composition, as a number of scholars have suggested (see note 23), and that the novel was not written in Toledo, as implied in the phrase "en *esta* insigne ciudad de Toledo," but somewhere else; the work, after all, is literature and not history.

The most productive investigations on the *Lazarillo* have been in the field of publication history. The scholarship of Alfredo Cavaliere,[27] José Caso González,[28] Francisco Rico,[29] and Alberto Blecua[30] have established a number of "facts" about the earliest editions of the novel: (1) none of the three 1554 texts—Antwerp, Burgos, and Alcalá—derive from any of the others; (2) there must have been at least two earlier printed editions, since Burgos derives from a lost text X and Antwerp and Alcalá from another lost text Y, which in turn most probably derived from X;[31] (3) these lost editions must have been printed in 1553, or, at the earliest, late 1552;[32] and (4) all the later editions (1555, 1573, 1587, 1595) positively derive from the Antwerp text.

Does the candidacy of Diego Hurtado de Mendoza fit into the schema created by these factual and hypothetical limitations? Many critics believe it does. *Lazarillo de Tormes* was first attributed to Mendoza in 1607 by V. A. Taxandrus (Valerii Andreae Taxandri) in his *Catalogus Clarorum Hispaniae Scriptorum* (44) and again a year later by Andrea Schott in *Hispaniae Bibliotheca* (543). Schott may have culled his information from his countryman, and he does not assert it as a fact but only as a belief *(putatur)*. Mendoza's authorship is also cited in a manuscript from the Madrid National Library (MS 9.752–53) entitled "Junta de libros la mejor que España ha visto en su lengua hasta el año 1624" by Tómas Tamayo de Vargas, but he may have also had access to Taxandrus or Schott. Finally, in the eighteenth century the great bibliographer Nicolás Antonio accepted Mendoza as the author of the book.

Don Diego's paternity reached its apex during the romantic period. In fact, all of the some dozen editions that appeared in the first half of the nineteenth century carried Mendoza's name on the frontispiece. The reason, however, was not due to any new facts that came to light, but because all the editors were following the same base text. A. Rumeau[33] has shown that an 1810 edition in Germany and an 1813 one in Paris put Mendoza as the author of the *Lazarillo* because of a statement to that effect in Bouterwek's influential history of Spanish Literature (1804, translated into French 1812), for which Bouterwek had probably consulted Nicolás Antonio, and that subsequent editions were based on the Paris text. In effect, the first scholar to dispute don Diego's paternity was A. Morel-Fatio in 1888 (see note 18).

Mendoza's candidacy was revived in the 1940s by Angel González Palencia.[34] Arguing more against Mendoza's detractors than for the humanist as the author, González Palencia proved that there were no reasons *not* to think that Mendoza wrote the novel. The Spanish scholar's efforts were continued by Erika Spivakovsky in three separate studies. In the first,[35] she noted that the same arguments used by M. J. Asensio (see note 18) to support Juan Valdés's authorship could be used more productively to support Mendoza's. In the second article,[36] she examined a letter with which Mendoza sent a satirical book of his to a nephew asking that the volume get to Philip II;[37] and she established a time table of events for Mendoza during the crucial years 1552–54: he left Italy in the autumn of 1552 for Charles's court in Germany and then in Brussels, he returned home by ship via England in the summer of 1553 and was probably in Alcántara from November to February 1554.

Spivakovsky also views the *Lazarillo* as autobiographical in that it parodies many of the events in Mendoza's life and some of the people with whom he worked; she thus sees, for example, the blindman as a parodic caricature of Pope Paul III and the young squire as a burlesque of Emperor Charles V. These observations are of course highly questionable, if not incredible. The same is true for her last study,[38] in which she argues unconvincingly that the *Lazarillo* is a parody of the life and fortunes of don Fernando Alvarez de Toledo (1507–82), the famous duke of Alba. He and Mendoza had been close friends during their youths. They had both attended the Cortes in 1525 (Alba was not at the 1538 parliament, although Mendoza was), and correspondence survives in which they remember those years in Toledo with joy. In 1549, however, the friendship between the two became strained due to differences of opinion concerning the political situation in Italy. While the above facts may be true, that by no means implies that the Lazarillo character is a parody of the duke of Alba.

During this same period other scholars were also examining the issue. Claudio Guillén spoke of "good reasons for thinking that don Diego Hurtado de Mendoza—humanist, diplomat, poet—could have written *Lazarillo*."[39] Donald McGrady proved conclusively that the author, whoever he was, necessarily had to be from the ranks of the nobility, since the only social class spared censure is that of the true nobles.[40] And Fred Abrams proposed the ingenious thesis that the first seven words of the novel—"Pues sepa Vuestra Merced ante todas cosas"[41]—contain the words *Urtado, Mendosa, Danteo,* and *Andrea;* such a precise rendition of don Diego's name and two pseudonyms were seen by Abrams to be more than mere coincidence.[42]

While the arguments of Spivakovsky and Abrams fail to convince, those of the eminent Hispanist Charles V. Aubrun do.[43] In a measured and carefully written study, Aubrun established that the work was written shortly before its publication in 1553–54; that the best edition is the Antwerp one, which indicates that the base text may have also been in Antwerp; that the author was evidently a mature, discreet, and prudent man; that he was not a professional writer, or he would have signed it; that he was not writing for money; that he was evidently a noble gentleman of the aristocracy; that he was a reform-minded person; and that he inserted items unfavorable to Emperor Charles V (the defeat at Jerba[44] and the oblique and bitter remark about the Cortes[45] which, if the one in 1525, may have to do with the uprising of the *Comuneros,* and if the one in 1538, may be very ironic). Into all of this fits the figure of only one person ever associated with the novel; don Diego Hurtado de Mendoza.

In summary, from what is known today, the authorship of *Lazarillo de Tormes* cannot be categorically resolved. There are sound arguments for rejecting certain attributions, such as those to the Valdés brothers, Lope de Rueda, and perhaps also Juan Ortega; but there are no reasons to assume that Sebastián de Horozco or Diego Hurtado de Mendoza did *not* write the book. Of the two, more is known about Mendoza and so he has a better case for paternity. He was in Toledo in 1525 and in 1538. He was in Flanders in 1552 and 1553 when and where the first printing of *Lazarillo* probably took place, and he was also in Spain in 1553–54 when the first Spanish editions appeared in Burgos and Alcalá de Henares. Furthermore, although Mendoza did not leave any work with his name on it that is exactly like the *Lazarillo,* he did write a number of satirical and parodic pieces. The tone and style of many of his letters is like that of the little book, and he is credited with the authorship of the "Carta al Capitán Salazar" and the "Diálogo entre Caronte y el ánima de Pedro Luis Farnesio," both written at about the same time as the supposed composition of the picaresque novel and both displaying the same critical spirit. In short, if the book is to be attributed to someone, there is no evidence to prove that don Diego could *not* have written it; yet, by the same token, there is no incontrovertible proof that Mendoza did indeed write *Lazarillo de Tormes.*

Chapter Five

Conclusion

Soldier, diplomat, imperial ambassador to England, Venice, and Rome, governor-general of Siena, naval administrator, state prisoner and exile: Diego Hurtado de Mendoza was all of these things at some time during his long career in service to the Spanish crown. He was on intimate terms with the most influential people in Europe: Charles V, Philip II, Henry VIII, popes Paul III and Julius III, the infamous duke of Alba, and many others. He lived in England for almost two years, in Venice for eight, and in Rome for five. He traveled extensively throughout Italy, Germany, Belgium, France, and his native Spain, and he was in Africa at least once. During the same period, his brothers were also acquiring responsibility and fame. Bernardino de Mendoza was the commander of the Spanish navy, Antonio was the viceroy of Mexico, Francisco was bishop of Jaen and later a cardinal. The Mendoza family was thus one of the most powerful and influential during the reign of Charles V, as indeed they had been for the preceding two hundred years.[1]

Poet, historian, classical archeologist, art collector, bibliophile, fluent in Spanish, Italian, Arabic, Latin, and ancient Greek: Diego Hurtado de Mendoza was also all of these things in Renaissance literary and artistic circles. He was a close friend of Juan Boscán and Garcilaso de la Vega, of Titian and Pietro Aretino, of Ambrosio Morales and Antonio Agustín, and he corresponded in verse and prose with these and many other outstanding European historians, poets, artists, and scholars.

Fortunately for posteriority, don Diego was an avid correspondent with virtually everyone he knew, and it is his letters that form the largest single body of written material by him. Indeed, Mendoza's correspondence is the largest corpus of Spanish letters by anyone outside of the royal family. Intimate to a fault, don Diego describes in his epistles everything from his own minor kidney infections to the most sophisticated diplomatic maneuvers taking place in sixteenth-century Europe. In the words of his biographer Erika Spivakovsky:

There is no contemporary of Mendoza (certainly no other Spaniard) whose reports of contact with foreign governments and peoples would offer an analogous illumination of the workings of power politics in the first post-Machiavellian decades. In the middle of the sixteenth century, the time of the Reformation, with its upheavals in the European balance of power between Spain, France, the Empire, the papacy, and smaller states, Mendoza's career provides a live commentary on the political events. The machinations of the rulers are revealed by his encounters—often detailed in his day-to-day proceedings—with the Senate of Venice, his government in Siena, the Duke of Florence, the Popes.[2]

In the realm of literature, don Diego is best known today as a historian and a poet. *Guerra de Granada,* his account of the tragic rebellion of the Christianized Arabs in his native Granada, is considered the best history of its kind to be written in sixteenth-century Spain. It is concise and truthful, stating the facts of the war in an unbiased and direct way that can only be described as modern. The more than twenty editions of *Guerra de Granada* that have appeared since 1627 are testimony to the work's value as a classic example of historical writing more than as a document for information concerning the Morisco rebellion.

Mendoza's poetry, while not as popular as that of his contemporaries Juan Boscán, Garcilaso de la Vega, Gutierre de Cetina, Baltasar del Alcázar, and Cristóbal de Castillejo, was justly appreciated during his lifetime. It received a fortunate renewal in popularity after the 1610 publication of his *Obras* by Juan Díaz Hidalgo, but fell into near oblivion until Adolfo de Castro republished both the poetry and some of the prose in the 1850s. Since then, Mendoza has received substantial attention by the critics, although his poetry appears only rarely in the anthologies of sixteenth-century literature.

There are some logical reasons for the neglect of Mendoza's poetry by Hispanist literary scholars. First, don Diego's liveliest verses are in imitation of classical models, and therefore not considered to be truly "poetic" in the modern, creative, sense of the word. Second, the bulk of his poetry, although much of it is in the revolutionary Italianate meters, still avows the clichéd courtly love psychology of the fifteenth-century *cancioneros.* It is therefore overlooked by critics in favor of the original verses of the preceding century. Third, none of Mendoza's poetry expresses the new Platonic mode of thought introduced by Boscán and Garcilaso, and later codified by Fernando de Herrera. Don Diego was a confirmed Aristotelian thinker all of his life,[3] and his poetry therefore does not fit well into the development from Bos-cán and Garcilaso through Herrera and Luis de León to Lope de Vega and Góngora that most scholars prefer to describe.[4] Fourth, the most original of don Diego's poetry is his Horatian epistles; and that genre of moral verse remains a neglected area of Hispanic scholarship for all of those who wrote it.[5] This volume hopefully will renew interest in Diego Hurtado de Mendoza's poetic works and will lead to proper recognition of his varied and substantial production.

Notes and References

Chapter One

1. The general information for this chapter has come from three studies, which will be hereafter cited by editors' / authors' last names in chapter
1 and in notes: Diego Hurtado de Mendoza, *Algunas cartas de don Diego Hurtado de Mendoza escritas 1538–1552*, ed. Alberto Vázquez and R. Selden Rose
(1935; reprint New York, 1973); Angel González Palencia and Eugenio
Mele, *Vida y obras de don Diego Hurtado de Mendoza*, 3 vols. (Madrid, 1941–
43); and Erika Spivakovsky, *Son of the Alhambra: Don Diego Hurtado de Mendoza, 1504–1575* (Austin, 1970).

2. For background on the Marqués de Santillana, see *Poesías completas*,
ed. Manuel Durán, 2 vols. (Madrid, 1975–80).

3. Many details of this conflict are outlined in my "The Awareness of
Higher Authority in *Fuenteovejuna*," in *Oelschläger Festschrift* (Chapel Hill,
1976), 143–49. See also Luis Suárez Fernández, *Nobleza y monarquía: Puntos
de vista sobre la historia castellana del siglo XV* (Valladolid, 1959).

4. See Lorenzo Riber, *El humanista Pedro Mártir de Anglería* (Barcelona, 1964).

5. Jerónimo Münzer, "Viaje por España y Portugal en los años 1494
y 1495, versión del Latin por Julio Puyol," *Boletín de la Real Academia de la
Historia* 84 (1924):87–88: "Finalmente entramos en la Alhambra. Pasando
por muchas puertas de hierro y por varias estancias de soldados y oficiales,
llegamos al noble y suntuosísimo palacio del alcaide don Iñigo López, conde
de Tendilla, de la casa castellana de Mendoza, quien habiendo leído la carta
que para él nos dió el alcaide de Almería, recibiónos con muchas muestras
de amor y amistad. Hablóme en Latín, porque es muy docto, y entendiéndole
perfectamente, le contesté en la misma lengua. Nos hizo sentar sobre telas
de seda; mandó traer un refresco, y luego, seguido de una lucida escolta de
soldados, nos acompañó en persona a visitar el real palacio, en el que vimos
salas con pavimento de blanquísimo mármol, jardines deleitosos con limo-
neros, arrayanes, estanques de marmóreos muros, cuatro habitaciones llenas
de armas, como son lanzas, ballestas, espadas, corazas y flechas; dormitorios
y tocadores; tazas de mármol con surtidores de agua en muchas salas, mayores
que la de San Agustín; una pieza de baños maravillosamente abovedada y,
adyacente a ella, un aposento con camas; altísimas columnas, un patio que
tiene en su centro una gran fuente de mármol sostenida por doce leones de
la misma piedra, que echan el agua por la boca como por caños; muchas losas
de quince pies de largo por siete u ocho de ancho, y otras cuadradas de diez
y once pies de lado. . . . No creo, en fin, que en Europa se halle nada seme-

jante, puesto que es todo tan magnífico, tan majestuoso, tan exquísitamente obrado, que ni el que lo contempla puede cerciorarse de que no está en un paraíso, ni a mí me sería posible hacer una relación exacta de cuanto vi. El conde nos acompañó constantemente, dándonos cumplidas explicaciones acerca de cada cosa."

6. José Cepeda Adán, "Andalucía en 1508," *Hispania* (Madrid) 22 (1962):32. See also Emilio Meneses García, *Correspondencia del conde de Tendilla*, 2 vols. (Madrid, 1972–74).

7. The best account in English of these events and their aftermath remains Henry Charles Lea, *The Moriscos of Spain* (1901; reprint, New York, 1968).

8. An excellent biography is Hayward Keniston, *Francisco de los Cobos, Secretary of the Emperor Carlos V* (Pittsburgh, 1959).

9. "Aviendo estudiado V. S. las tres lenguas, Latina, Griega y Aráviga en Granada y Salamanca, y después allí los derechos civil y canónico; y aviendo andado buena parte de España para ver y sacar fielmente las piedras antiguas della, se passó en Italia, donde siguiendo la guerra, en el grado que su persona merecía, assí repartía el tiempo del año, que asistiendo los veranos en la guerra, los inviernos se iba a Roma y a Padua y a otras universidades donde había insignes maestros, como eran Agustín Nypho, Montesdoca y otros para oírles lógica, philosophía y mathemáticas" (González Palencia and Mele, 3: 472).

10. "un hombre de armas de la compañía de don Diego de Mendoza . . ." (*BAE*, vol. 81 [Madrid, 1955], 87). Sandoval consistently refers to the ambassador as simply don Diego de Mendoza: *BAE*, 82 (Madrid, 1956), 383 and passim.

11. Both letters have been published by R. Foulché-Delbosc, "Cartas de Don Diego Hurtado de Mendoza," *Archivo de Investigaciones Históricas* 2 (1911):193, 537.

12. R. Trevor Davies, *The Golden Century of Spain, 1501–1621* (New York, 1965), 97.

13. *Guerra de Granada*, ed. Bernardo Blanco-González (Madrid, 1970), 96: "Será lo que hallé en los libros arábigos de la tierra, y los de Muley Hacen rey de Túnez."

14. A muster list published in *Colección de Documentos Inéditos para la Historia de España* 16 (1850):252, mentions "Hurtado de Mendoza id." as commanding a Spanish company of two hundred and fifteen men.

15. See Vázquez and Rose, ix–xi; Spivakovsky, 60–68; and González Palencia and Mele, 1: 71–86.

16. Castro knew of the affair, since reference is made to it in *The Structure of Spanish History*, trans, Edmund L. King (Princeton, 1954), 251; although he also noted Mendoza's comments were "either in jest or in earnest."

17. In *BAE* 32: 44–45.
18. Mendoza's translation was published by R. Foulché-Delbosc, *"Mechánica de Aristóteles," Revue Hispanique* 5 (1898):365–405.
19. *Allegatione o vera protesta fatta per l'illustriss. S. D. Diego de Mendoza, Ambiasciatore della Cesarea Maestá al S. di N. S. Papa Pauolo III sopra le cose appartenente al Concilio generale di Trento* (Milan, 1548).
20. "Las causas porque me partí fueron por dar quenta de mis acciones a V. A., porque ya a S. M. no tenía obligación como criado, porque ministros dijeron que S. M. no se servía más de mí, porque me exluyó S. M. de algunos cargos, para que fui nombrado, con palabras poco convenientes a sí y a mí, porque no quedó por S. M. habiéndole servido veintidós años de quitarme la reputación y aun la honra si pudiera, y al tiempo que esperaba gratificación y remuneración, traerme a términos de justificación.

"Porque S. M. ha hecho conmigo solo lo que con criado ministro, y esto sin causa y a instancia de mis enemigos, de lo que estoy y viviré muy sentido y agraviado perpetuamente quanto S. M. y yo viviéremos, no me reparando la ofensa que me ha hecho. Porque S. M. no me hizo más merced de la que bastó para cubrirse a sí mismo de la imputación que el mundo le podía dar, siendo éstos mis descargos y mi inocencia, y yo no tenía posibilidad ni voluntad de seguir por entonces a S. M." (González Palencia and Mele, 2:289).
21. Spivakovsky, 333–35. These facts were hotly contested by J. O. Scrouch, "El autor del *Lazarillo* sobre una reciente tesis," *Hispanófila* 19 (1963):11–23, when responding to two earlier studies by Spivakovsky: *Hispanófila* 12 (1961):15–23 and *Symposium* 15 (1961):271–85. Spivakovsky offers additional data to substantiate her dates in *Son of the Alhambra.*
22. R. Foulché-Delbosc, "Correspondencia de doña Magdalena de Bobadilla," *Revue Hispanique* 8 (1901):1–59.
23. *Obras poéticas,* ed. William Knapp (Madrid, 1877), 332–39; hereafter cited in the text as *OP*.
24. "Dióme también V. S. con insigne liberalidad todas las monedas antiguas que tenía de tiempo de Romanos, con nombres de lugares de España, y copias y relaciones de inscripciones raras, que por ella se hallan y me ayudarán mucho en lo que yo aquí he de tratar, como en el discurso de la obra se verá. Y si yo había de buscar quien bien juzgase de lo mucho que en esto se ha trabajado y descubierto, ¿quién puede hazer la estima deste mi trabajo como V. S. que tan singularmente entiende todo lo de las antigüedades Romanas?; teniendo junto con esto tanta noticia y tan particular de las de España, que todos lo que algo dessean saber, y con razón piensan que saben algo en ellas, reconocen en V. S. un señorío y excelencia grande en saberlas y averlas con mucho ingenio, diligenia y juicio averiguado. . . .

"Y porque V. S. con sus grandes cargos residía en diversos lugares, y su librería era en todos tan grande, que no podía nadie tan presto mudarse,

tomaba otros códices nuevos de los autores que más amaba y bolvíalos a pas-
sar, como si antes no los uviera passado. Assí se ven en su librería, agora que
está toda junta, dos y tres obras de unos mismos autores, rayadas y notadas
de su mano. Porque el leer y estudiar era siempre el mayor entretenimiento
de V. S.: éste era el descansar de negocios y aliviar de trabajos.

"Deste grande amor que V. S. ha tenido a las letras, ha resultado el
singular provecho de tener, como tenemos, tantos y tantos insignes autores
Griegos, que antes no teníamos; pues como hizo traer de Grecia muchas cosas
de los santos Basilio, Gregorio Nacianzeno, Cyrilo, y de otros excelentes autores, de todo Arquímedes, mucho de Herón, de Appiano Alexandrino y de
otros. Y en la manera de haberlos avido, ay otra singular alabança; porque
aviendo V. S. enbiádole al gran Turco Soliymán libremente y sin ningún res-
cate un su cativo, aquel gran señor le mandó dezir que pidiesse todo lo que
quisiesse. Entonces V. S. le pidió dos cosas dignísimas de su grandeza y amor
a las letras. Pidióle saca de trigo para los Venecianos, que padecían gran ham-
bre a la sazón, y libros de los que avía en Grecia. Assí con aver dado la saca
de trigo muy abundante, enbió a V. S. seys caxas de libros y más verdadera-
mente de inestimables tesoros de sabiduría" (González Palencia and Mele,
3:470–73).

25. "Y porque yo tengo cuentas con el Rey nuestro señor, en las cuales
me ponen dudas, aunque el Rey muy bien entiende que no soy alcanzado;
por sanear mi conciencia y mi lealtad, hago a su Magestad mi universal he-
redero y suplico le nombre por executor deste mi inventario y lo mando cum-
plir al pie de la letra, que sobran bienes" (González Palencia and Mele,
2:389).

26. "Den dritten ist der könig nach dem Pardo verruckt. Den neinten
ist der don Diego de Mendoza, in ganzer welt wol bekannt, erkrankt, darzue
ihm spasmus in ain schenkl geschlagen, dermaßen man ihn denselben under
dem knie abnemen muessen, welches er in ansehung er über sibenzig jar alt
gewest, nicht übersteen könn, sonder ist den dreizehenden Christlich gestor-
ben" (Hans Khevenhüller, *Geheimes Tagebuch 1548–1605*, ed. Georg Kheven-
hüller-Metch and Günther Probszt-Ohstorff [Graz, 1971], 87). I am grateful
to Professor Spivakovsky for bringing this work to my attention.

27. "Diga a S. M. que todo era por sauer lo que ordena de la librería,
y como el testamento es cerrado no lo he podido sauer, pero vi por allí
muchos libros y mucha gente y podrá ser, aun sin podrá ser, que cuando se
quiera recoger no haya qué, y por esto sería bien dar alguna traza; ésta podría
dar S. M. como quien tan buenas las tiene, y v. m., y mandarme avisar,
porque sentiría mucho se perdiese una hoja de papel de los que tiene"
(González Palencia and Mele, 2:391).

28. "En acabando de recibir y concertar la librería de don Diego de
Mendoza haré un índice general de toda la de S. M. y le imprimiré, porque
creo será cosa de ver en donde quiera que parezca" (González Palencia and
Mele, 2: 394).

Chapter Two

1. The translation of this piece comes from appendix B of my *Juan Boscán* (Boston, 1978), 136–39.

2. Luis Zapata, *Memorial Histórico Español*, vol. II (Madrid, 1859): "los canonizados buenos escritores" (141); "los muy caballeros de quien hoy corre la sangre de la tinta fresca, y correrá para siempre, Boscán y Garcilaso; Don Diego de Mendoza . . . (142).

3. In his translation of Petrarch's *Triumphs* (Salamanca, 1581): "tantos, como los que en el día de hoy son de voto que al pie de la letra se imita también en esto la manera del verso italiano, como en todas las otras cosas; puesto caso que no es justo que ninguno condene por malo aquello que don Diego de Mendoza, y el secretario Gonzalo Pérez, y don Juan de Coloma, y Garcilaso de la Vega, y Juan Boscán y otras muchas personas doctas tienen aprobado por bueno" (González Palencia and Mele, 3:234).

4. Fernández de Velasco's statement is in *Observaciones del licenciado Prete Jacopín contra las Anotaciones de Herrera a las obras de Garcilaso* ("Pues sus coplas redondillas es cosa cierta que no tienen par") and Lope's is in the *Isidro* ("¿Qué cosa aventaja a una redondilla de Garci Sánchez o de don Diego de Mendoza?"). Both are cited by González Palencia and Mele, 3:229.

5. From his *Anotaciones a Garcilaso*, in Antonio Gallego Morell, *Garcilaso de la Vega y sus comentaristas* (Universidad de Granada, 1966), 642: "El ingenioso caballero Don Diego de Mendoza, ¿qué quiso decir, que no pudiese en sus coplas castellanas?"

6. "Don Diego de Mendoza halló maravillosamente y trató sus conceptos, que llaman del ánimo, y todas sus perturbaciones con más espíritu que cuidado y alcanzó con novedad lo que pretendió siempre, que fue apartarse de la común senda de los otros poetas, y satisfecho con ello se olvidó de las demás cosas; porque si como tuvo en todo lo que escribió erudiciones y espíritu y abundancia de sentimientos, quisiera servirse de la pureza y elegancia en la lengua, y componer el número y suavidad de los versos, no tuviéramos envidia a los mejores en otras lenguas peregrinas. Y no se puede dejar de conceder, que cuando reparó con algún cuidado, ninguno le hizo ventaja, pero como él se ejercitó por ocupar horas ociosas, o librar el ánimo de otros cuidados molestos, así el natural donaire y viveza de sus versos lo desvían, como tengo dicho, del vulgo de la poesía común" (Gallego Morell, *Garcilaso y sus comentaristas*, 289–90).

7. "En sus obras de burlas (que por dignos respectos aquí no se ponen) mostró tener agudeza y donayre, siendo satírico sin infamia agena, mezclando lo dulce con lo prouechoso. La zanahoria, cana, pulga, y otras cosas burlescas, que por su gusto, o por el de sus amigos compuso, por no contrauenir a la grauedad de tan insigne Poeta, no se dan a la estampa: y por esto, que ya por no ser tan comunes, serán más estimadas de quien las tenga, y las conozca" (*OP*, xxviii–xxix).

8. The best general introduction to love in the *cancioneros* remains Otis H. Green, "Courtly Love in the Spanish *Cancioneros*," *PMLA* 64 (1949):247–301.

9. Malcolm C. Batchelor, *"A ti, Doña Marina": The Poetry of Don Diego Hurtado de Mendoza* (Havana, 1959), 50; follows the autograph manuscript, Esp. 311, in Bibliothèque Nationale, Paris.

10. Extensive research has been done on doña Marina by A. Morel-Fatio, *Etudes sur l'Espagne*, 3rd ser. (Paris, 1904), 77–87; and J. P. W. Crawford, "Notes on the Poetry of Diego Hurtado de Mendoza," *Modern Language Review* 23 (1928):36–51.

11. See my "Garcilaso's Love for Isabel Freire: The Creation of a Myth," *Journal of Hispanic Philology* 3 (1979): 261–68.

12. "Mais il fout aussi se mefier du style poétique de l'époque, il faut éviter d'être dupe d'un langage conventionnel que n'a que trop sevi depuis Petrarque dans la poésie italienne et, a son exemple, dans la poésie espagnole. En l'absence d'autres témoignages plus probantes, laissons donc dans la pénombre, dans un vague mystérieux, les relations de don Diego et de doña Marina" (*Etudes sur l'Espagne*, 86).

13. Mitchell D. Triwedi, "On Mendoza's Sonnet to His Book," *Romance Notes* 12 (1970–71):413–15.

14. "The anxiety of the imperiled mariner casting anchor into the sea suggests the anxiety of the lovesick poet sending forth his book to his beloved. . . . Thus the sonnet ends with a reinforcement of the *galardón* motif implicit in the concluding hemistitch of the octave" ("On Mendoza's Sonnet," 415).

15. Otis H. Green, *Spain and the Western Tradition*, vol. 1 (Madison, 1963), whose entire content is devoted to courtly love.

16. The opposite occurs in Boscán's poetry. Both he and Garcilaso evidently ceased using Castilian meters when they turned to Italian forms; and both poets also evolved poetically from the courtly love rhetoric to a Platonic concept of love. See my *Juan Boscán*.

17. Sonnet 5, "En la fuente más clara y apartada," is a bright, limpid poem that describes a pastoral ambience in which doña Marina is a female Apollo seated by a fountain with the seven muses. It is definitely not in the courtly mold.

18. José María de Cossío, *Fábulas mitológicas en España* (Madrid, 1952), says of Mendoza's "Fábula de Adonis, Hipómenes y Atalanta": "Este poema, aún mejor que el de Boscán, puede decirse que abre el camino en la poesía española a esta clase de paráfrasis mitológicas" (97).

19. From the introduction to his translation of Boethius's *De consolatione philosophiae*. In reference to his own translation, he says it is "sin las borlas de don Diego de Mendoza, que decía que las traducciones eran de la condición de los tapices vueltos al revés, que descubrían las figuras, pero llenas de borlas y de hilachas" (cited in Cossío, *Fábulas mitológicas*, 63).

20. Marcelino Menéndez Pelayo praises the "Fábula" as "un poemita en octavas reales, que es sin disputa, el mejor de sus ensayos en el metro italiano" (*Obras de Lope de Vega*, vol. 13 [*BAE*, 187:208–9]).

21. See González Palencia and Mele, 119–22.

22. *Carta*, ed. Castro, 73.

23. *The Metamorphoses*, trans. Horace Gregory (New York, 1955), 407.

24. Ibid., 405.

25. Ibid., 406.

26. Irving P. Rothberg, "Hurtado de Mendoza and the Green Epigrams," *Hispanic Review* 26 (1958): 171–87; but see also his "The Greek Anthology in Spanish Poetry 1500–1700" (Ph.D. diss., Pennsylvania State, 1954).

27. González Palencia and Mele, 3:56, cite as the source for "A Venus" Ausonius's epigram 64: "Armatum vidit Venerem Lacedemone Pallas. / 'Nunc certemus, ait, iudice vel Paride.' / Cui Venus: 'armatum tu me, temeraria, temnis, / quae, quo te vici tempore, nuda fui?' "; and as the source for "A Lais" epigram 65: "Lais anus Veneri speculum dico: dignum habeat se / aeterna aeternum forma ministerium. / At mihi nullus in hoc usus, quia cernere talem, / qualis sum nolo, qualis eram, nequeo."

28. *The Greek Anthology*, trans. W. R. Paton (London and New York, 1926), 5:261: "Pallas, seeing Cytherea in arms, said 'Cypris, wouldst thou that we went to judgment so?' But she, with a gentle smile, answered, 'Why should I lift up a shield in combat? If I conquer when naked, how will it be when I arm myself?' "

29. See Edgar Wind, *Pagan Mysteries in the Renaissance* (New York, 1968), 81–96.

30. "Pompeios iuvenes Asia atque Europa, sed ipsum / terra tegit Libyes, si tamen ulla tegit. / Quid mirum todo si spargitur orbe? iacere / uno non poderat tanta ruina loco" (in Anthony A. Giulan, *Martial and the Epigram in Spain in the Sixteenth and Seventeenth Centuries* [Philadelphia, 1930], 22).

31. The section in question is the forty-five lines "No me curo del cetro del tirano, / . . . / Y a tí te cabrá parte del sabor." It comes from the *Planudean Anthology* epigrams 11.47 ("I care not for the wealth of Cyges the king of Sardis, nor does gold take me captive, and I praise not tyrants. I care to drench my beard with scent and crown my head with roses. I care for to-day, who knows to-morrow?" [*Greek Anthology*, trans. Paton, 4:93]) and 11.48 ("Moulding the silver make me, Hephaestus, no suit of armour, but fashion as deep as thou canst a hollow cup, and work on it neither stars nor chariots nor hateful Orion, but blooming vines and laughing clusters with lovely Bacchus" [*Greek Anthology*, trans. Paton, 4:93]). González Palencia and Mele, 3:88–91, mistakenly thought the section derived from an anacreontic poem in the *Noctes Atticae* of Aulus Gellius. Cf. Rothberg, "Hurtado de Mendoza," 175.

32. The *locus classicus* is the *Planudean Anthology* poem 9.44 (*Greek Anthology*, trans. Paton, 3:25); but Mendoza probably used Luigi Alamanni's Italian version of Ausonius's Latin version of the Greek poem: "Un che impiccarsi per povertà intende, / Trova un tesoro, lascia il laccio, il prende; / L'altro che il suo tesor trova furato, / Impicca se col laccio ivi trovato" (in Rothberg, "Hurtado de Mendoza," 179).

33. González Palencia and Mele, 3:85: "Las poesías más perfectas de Mendoza, porque iluminan la vida interior del poeta."

34. Elias L. Rivers, "The Horatian Epistle and Its Introduction into Spanish Literature," *Hispanic Review* 22 (1954):182.

35. D. J. Palmer, "The Verse Epistle," in *Metaphysical Poetry*, ed. Malcolm Bradbury and David Palmer (Bloomington, 1971), 74.

36. Ibid., 83.

37. For a comparison of Mendoza's poem with Boscán's reply, see Rivers, "The Horatian Epistle," 175–94; Arnold G. Reichenberger, "Boscán's *Epístola a Mendoza*," *Hispanic Review* 17 (1949):1–17; and David H. Darst, *Juan Boscán*, 99–109.

38. "Nil admirari res est una, Numici, / solaque quae possit facere et servare beatum. / Hunc solem et stellas et decedentia certis / tempora momentis sunt qui formidine nulla / imbuti spectent. Quid censes munera terrae? / quid maris extremos Arabas ditantis et Indos?" (*The Epistles of Horace*, ed. Augustus S. Wilkins, [London, 1964], 13).

39. "Qui timet his adversa, fere miratur eodem / quo cupiens pacto: pavor est utrobique molestus, / improvisa simul species exterret utrumque. / Gaudeat an doleat, cupiat metuatne, quid ad rem, / si, quicquid vidit melius peiusque sua spe, / defixis oculis animoque et corpore torpet? Insani sapiens nomen ferat, aequus iniqui, ultra quam satis est virtutem si petat ipsam" (*Epistles*, ed. Wilkins, 13–14).

40. "Yo, Boscán, no procuro otro tesoro / sino poder vivir medianamente, / ni escondo la riqueza ni la adoro. / Si aquí hallas algún inconveniente, / como discreto, y no como yo soy, / me desengaña dello incontinente, / y si no, ven conmigo adonde voy" (*OP*, 115).

41. Rivers, "The Horatian Epistle," 191.

42. Adolfo de Castro, *BAE*, 32:56, entitles it "A don Luis de Zuñiga." The diplomatic career and writings of this close friend of don Diego have been exhaustively studied by A. González Palencia, *Don Luis de Zuñiga y Avila* (Madrid, 1932).

43. González Palencia / Mele dedicated only three lines to *Carta* 3: "En la tercera epístola, A don Luis de Avila, es notable el pasaje en que se alude a Carlos V: "Tú sirve al gran señor . . . " (3:88).

44. Batchelor, *"A ti Doña Marina,"* 45.

45. Mendoza's sonnet is almost a literal translation of his source: "Littore dum phario prima Saladinus in olga / Barbara deuicto castra oriente locat. / Venit adulatrix regum comes unica turba / Et quibus ut lingua promp-

tior unus erat. / Nunc domitam aegiptum iactat: nunc littora rubra / tractaque pugnaci gallica sceptra manu, / ostentatque uirum duris tot milia in armis. / Et iubet hinc uires aestimet ipse suas, / Scilicet hinc ille: Atque adeo ex hac, infit, arena / Quae te semiustum littore, Magne, tenet" (in González Palencia and Mele, 3:108).

46. Marullo uses the name Enyo for the goddess of war, more commonly known as Bellona: "Cuius hic in tumulus? Quae tu rogo? et unde uerendas / Tunsa genas crinem sic laniata sedes. / Annibalis cinerem sacrum aspicis; ast ego, Enyo, / Fada uiri, et casus hic queror immeritos. / Quem Roma deuicta odio inuidiaque suorum / Tam procul a Libya terra Libyssa tegit. / Non tamen Annibalis opera nisi et ense superbo, / Annibalem potuit perdere parca noiens" (in González Palencia and Mele, 3:109).

47. Alciati's *Emblemata* was translated into Spanish in 1549 and again in 1615. Two excellent studies on Spanish emblems are Giuseppina Ledda, *Contributo allo studio della letteratura emblematica in Spagna (1549–1613)* (Pisa, 1970), and Aquilino Sánchez Pérez, *La literatura emblemática española (siglos XVI y XVII)* (Madrid, 1977).

48. The Latin is equally jestful and conceitful: "Errabat socio Mors iuncta Cupidine: secum / Mors pharetras, parvus tela gerebat Amor. / Divertere simul, simul una nocte cubarunt: / caecus Amor, Mors hoc tempore caeca fuit. / Alter enim alterius male provida spicula sumpsit, / Mors aurata, tenet orsea tela Puer. / Debuit inde senex qui nunc Acheronticus esse, / ecce amat, et capiti florea serta parat. / At ego, mutato quia Amor me percutit arcu, / deficio, injiciunt et mihi fata manum. / Parce, Puer: Mors signa tenes victricia, parce: / fac ego amem; subeat fac Acheronte senex!" (in González Palencia and Mele, 3:106–7).

49. "Cum Nero in exitium properaret matris apertum, / dicitur hac natum voce rogasse parens: / Non oculos, non ora petas: pete viscera ferro; / viscera tam magnum quae peperere nefas" (in Rothberg, "Hurtado de Mendoza," 180).

50. *Opera* (Basel, 1544), 275. Quoted by G. W. Pigman III, "Versions of Imitation in the Renaissance," *Renaissance Quarterly* 33 (1980):18. Referring to Calcagnini's letter, Pigman notes: "Forms of *certo* and *contendo* are generally used to advocate *aemulatio*, often in opposition to forms of *sequor*, a major term for imitation when not used to indicate a third kind of imitation called following. A cluster of images associated with the paths—*via* (or *callis* or a similar word), *dux, vestigium*—comprise the other class of eristic metaphor. Both classes are used to support both imitation and emulation, depending on the theorist's view of competition and the possibility of successful competition" (19).

51. Pigman, "Versions of Imitation," 32.

52. "El sentido de continuidad, sobre cuya base puede eficazmente desenvolverse con toda su fuerza el mito de los clásicos; la corriente de emulación, suscitada por la reconocida ejemplaridad de aquéllos; el despertar de la

conciencia histórica que permite distinguir y comparar épocas y grupos humanos; el sentimiento de comunidad política que, renovado bajo la influencia de los antiguos en forma de patriotismo, compromete a la defensa e ilustración del propio grupo; la preferencia por los modernos que, a través de tan larga polémica, se afirma como fruto del Renacimiento; la confianza en la experiencia personal y la autonomía de la razón, con su abierta y amplia crítica del principio de autoridad: tales son los factores que en la crisis del siglo XVI, sobre la base de las nuevas condiciones socio-económicas que trae consigo el crecimiento de la burguesía, se desarrollan y articulan para dar origen a la teoría del progreso como visión general del curso de la historia" (*Antiguos y modernos* [Madrid, 1966], 477–78).

53. "Para la primera doctrina humanista de la imitación, el logro de una versión moderna que pueda confundirse con una obra antigua es motivo de la mayor admiración. Para el humanista tardío, más provisto de conciencia histórica y que, fundado en ella, no pretende confundirse con los antiguos, la admiración por los productos que la cultura de éstos nos ha legado se mantiene en tanto que son auténticos. . . . De la misma manera, el investigador o el coleccionista no pretenden una restauración de los antiguos. Ellos son unos modernos que estudian el pasado desde su tiempo, instalados en éste conscientemente, situación de la que fácilmente deriva una mayor autoestimación" (*Antiguos y modernos*, 419–20).

54. "Si el Humanismo renacentista tenía tal vez como primera de sus marcas la veneración por el latín y por el griego, ese mismo Humanismo suscitaría el interés y, finalmente, la exaltación honrosa de la lengua propia. El proceso ya nos es conocido. Se inicia con una primera fase en actitud de puro acatamiento a las lenguas clásicas, para postular después un mejoramiento de la lengua vulgar, por imitación de aquéllas, y llegar finalmente a buscar en el propio ser y contextura de cada lengua presente la norma de su desarrollo y perfeccionamiento—perfección que, antes de que termine el siglo XVI, muchos consideran haber sido ya alcanzada—, hasta el punto de poderse colocar la lengua vulgar y la obra de los 'auctores' que en ella escriben por encima de cuantos dejó en herencia la antigüedad" (*Antiguos y modernos*, 499).

Chapter Three

1. *Guerra de Granada*, ed. Blanco-González; hereafter cited in the text.

2. "La estudiosidad de la historia suele ser la madre más feliz de la Prudencia, y la que le pare con menos dolor. Ella con ayuda de un reparo observante y reflexo sobre los acaecimientos presentes, notando los errores y precipicios de lo passado, sabe prevenir y burlar los imminentes y convertir en aciertos los peligros. Sin esto no creo que se pueda ni posseer la Prudencia adquirida ni reynar con alabança" (Francisco Garau, *Tercera parte del Sabio, instruido de la naturaleza* [Madrid, 1710], 230). For a full survey of this topic

see David H. Darst, "The Persistence of the Exemplum in Spanish Golden Age Thought," *Renaissance and Reformation* 9 (1973):58–64.

3. "Historia y experiencia son dos aspectos de una misma realidad, y una y otra son, para el hombre del XVI y XVII, recíprocamente reversibles; la historia es experiencia, la experiencia historia" (Enrique Tierno Galván, *El tacitismo en las doctrinas políticas del siglo de oro español* [Murcia, 1949], 55).

4. "Tienen otro bien las historias que mediante ellas podemos dezir somos viejos, pues sabemos lo que pudiéramos saber si fuéramos nacidos en aquellos tiempos que sucedieron" (Luis Alfonso de Carballo, *Cisne de Apolo*, ed. Alberto Porqueras Mayo [Madrid, 1958], 2:47).

5. Cervantes, *Persiles y Sigismunda*: "Las lecciones de los libros muchas veces hacen más cierta experiencia de las cosas, que no la tienen los mismos que las han visto, a causa que el que lee con atención repara una y muchas veces en lo que va leyendo, y con este excede a la lección la vista" (bk. 3, chap. 8).

6. "Con la memoria de las cosas passadas y que en otros tiempos han succedido, se ve a los que puede acaescer en los tiempos venideros, y en los hechos, y acaescimientos del mundo, vemos que los casos y cosas que succeden, por la mayor parte, son semejantes a las que ya en otros tiempos acaescieron" (Tomas Cerdán de Tallada, *Verdadero govierno desta monarchia* [Valencia, 1581], folios 15ᵛ–16ʳ).

7. "Quien quiere antever lo que ha de sucederle, deve estudiar en las historias lo que en otros reynados sucedió. Porque en los acontecimientos humanos, si se passan los siglos y los individuos se mudan, las causas y los sucessos o son muy parecidos o los mismos. Passan y se mudan contínuamente las aguas; pero siempre se queda el mismo río. No siempre son los mismos los que son Vassallos y Reyes; pero siempre son Reyes los que mandan y Vassallos los que obedecen: y en lo que passó en los passados deve prevenirse lo que passará en los presentes: Si aquí concurren y se cevan las causas que allí obraron, ¿cómo no han de producir los mismos efectos?" (Francisco Garau, *Tercera parte del Sabio*, 232–33).

8. This point is admirably substantiated by Maravall, *Antiguos y modernos* 395–96.

9. See Peter Burke, *The Renaissance Sense of the Past* (New York, 1969), especially chap. 4, "Historical Explanation," 77–104; and Myron P. Gilmore, "Individualism in Renaissance Historians," in *Humanists and Jurists: Six Studies in the Renaissance* (Cambridge, Mass., 1963), 38–60.

10. "En el siglo XVII se inicia una visión de la Historia que concibe ésta como el depósito de imperfecciones y de errores que hay que superar. Ella nos muestra, dice Saavedra Fajardo, 'cómo fueron las acciones de los gobiernos pasados para enmienda de los presentes'; más aún, si aquella 'es una representación de las edades del mundo,' de tal manera que 'por ella la memoria vive los días de los pasados,' la consecuencia es que 'los errores de los que ya fueron advierten a los que son' " (*Antiguos y modernos*, 396–97).

11. "La lección de la propia historia ser a cada nación más provechosa y grata que la extranjera consta manifiestamente" (ibid., 417).

12. Gilmore, "The Renaissance Conception of the Lessons of History," in *Humanists and Jurists*, 18.

13. Herrera's philosophy of history has been thoroughly examined by Mary Gaylord Randel, *The Historical Prose of Fernando de Herrera* (London, 1971).

14. Burke, *Renaissance Sense of the Past*, 105.

15. Ibid., 105–30.

16. Ibid., 106.

17. "Voluntariamente oscuro y reticente," "recortado y sentencioso": in Julio Caro Baroja, *Ciclos y temas de la historia de España: Los moriscos del Reino de Granada (ensayo de historia social)*, 2d ed. (Madrid, 1976), 31, 181.

18. Burke, *Renaissance Sense of the Past*, 106.

19. See Lea, *The Moriscos of Spain*, 20–21.

20. Mendoza's father's career is detailed in Helen Nader, *The Mendoza Family in the Spain Renaissance 1350–1550* (New Brunswick, 1979), chapter 6, "Open Conflict: Tendilla versus the Letrados" (150–79).

21. Helen Nader (in ibid.) sees this conflict as the culmination of a two hundred year struggle between the regionalistic aristocratic *caballero* humanists and the imperialistic scholarly *letrado* lawyers. The first—typified by the Mendoza family—were military men in favor of diffused monarchical power. The second—typified by legal scholars trained in the scholastic schools outside Spain—were professional bureaucrats in favor of a central monarchical power. The first wrote history in the vernacular and were interested in Castilian literature, while the second wrote political propaganda in Latin and were interested in classical literature. Finally, the *caballeros* sought always to separate state and church, secular authority and religious authority, but the *letrados*, who won the conflict, were the formulators of the new Castilian religious policy of lay reform.

22. See Davies, *The Golden Century of Spain*, 171–72.

23. A. C. Hess, "The Moriscos: An Ottoman Fifth Column in Sixteenth Century Spain," *American Historical Review* 74 (1968–69): 13.

24. Davies, *The Golden Century of Spain*, 170. See also J. H. Elliott, *Imperial Spain 1469–1716* (New York, 1966), 227–28.

25. For corroborative evidence, see the detailed study of K. Garrad, "La Inquisición y los moriscos granadinos," *Bulletin Hispanique* 67 (1965):63–77.

26. By Gaspar Ibáñez de Segovia, about 1696. Parts of the manuscript, which is in Madrid's Biblioteca Nacional, have been published by A. Morel-Fatio, *L'Espagne au XVIe et au XVIIe siècle* (Paris, 1878), 66–96.

27. "Cuando llegó a ocupar la misma presidencia don Pedro de Deza, fue tal la hostilidad entre los Mendoza y él, que el autor de la *Historia de la*

casa de Mondéjar no vacila en afirmar que la sublevación de los moriscos fue originada por ella: 'Procedió—he aquí sus palabras—de la emulación y competencias entre el Capitán General y la Chancillería cuyo Presidente, don Pedro Deça, para estender su Jurisdicción y disminuir la militar, que hasta entonces havía tenido la superintendencia de todos los Moriscos del Reyno, persuadió al Rey convenía promulgar diversas Premáticas moderando los excesos de sus costumbres, de sus trajes y de sus juntas, para que le tocase a él, y a la Chancillería, el conocimiento y castigo de su contravención' " (Caro Baroja, *Los moriscos del Reino de Granada*, 151–52).

28. See also Caro Baroja, *Los moriscos del Reino de Granada*, 158–59; and Lea, *The Moriscos of Spain*, 229.

29. Documented by James T. Monroe, "A Curious Morisco Appeal to the Ottoman Empire," *Al-Andalus* 31 (1966):281–303.

30. The Granadan Moriscos in the Albaicín and the surrounding Vega never did rebel. The war was from the beginning essentially a rural one; for it was the farming and silk industry that was most affected by the new taxes and economic sanctions included in the revised Edict of 1526, and it was the rural folk who had most resisted acculturation and who therefore were most persecuted by the religious authorities. See the important study of Antonio Domínguez Ortiz and Bernard Vincent, *Historia de los moriscos: Vida y tragedia de una minoría* (Madrid, 1978), esp. 47.

31. Mendoza had introduced Vélez in book 1. His statements there and here in book 2 highlight the enmity between the house of Mondéjar and the Vélez family: "With the present danger mitigated, the president, either beginning to think more freely about serving the king or from jealousy of the Marqués de Mondéjar, wrote to don Luis Fajardo, Marqués de Vélez, who was govenor of Murcia and captain-general of Cartagena, . . . urging him to gather an army and enter through Almería, where he would do a service for the king, he would succor that city which was in danger from sea and land, *and his people would profit from the enemy's riches.* The Marqués was held to be spirited and diligent, and between him and the Marqués de Mondéjar there were always differences and ill-will extending from their parents and grandparents" (136).

32. Domínguez Ortiz and Vincent, *Historia de los moriscos*, 55.

33. For a fascinating account of the life and works of this man, see Darío Carbanelas Rodríguez, *El morisco granadino Alonso del Castillo* (Granada, 1965).

34. Henri Lepeyre, *Géographie de l'Espagne morisque* (Paris, 1959), 125.

35. Domínguez Ortiz and Vincent, *Historia de los moriscos*, 52.

36. Ibid., 56.

37. Ibid., 83.

38. Ibid., 208–9.

39. Spivakovsky, 400.

40. Consult the lists compiled by Blanco-González, 71–74; and José Simón Díaz, *Bibliografía de la literatura hispánica*, vol. 11 (Madrid, 1976), nos. 5647–74.

41. Readily available in *Biblioteca de Autores Españoles*, vol. 21 (*Historiadores de sucesos particulares*).

42. For corroboration, see B. Sánchez Alonso, "La literatura histórica en el siglo XVI," *Historia general de las literaturas hispánicas*, vol. 3 (Barcelona, 1953), 310–11.

43. Other popular treatises were Pedro Cardona Aznar, *Expulsión justificada de los moriscos españoles* (Huesca, 1612), Damián Fonseca, *Justa expulsión de los moriscos de España* (Roma, 1611), and Marcos de Guadalajara y Javier, *Memorable expulsión y justísimo destierro de los moriscos de España* (Pamplona, 1613).

44. María Soledad Carrasco-Urgoiti, *The Moorish Novel* (Boston, 1976), 124–36.

45. See Gilmore, *Humanists and Jurists*, 56–58.

46. Part of this chapter appeared earlier as the article "El pensamiento histórico del granadino Diego Hurtado de Mendoza," *Hispania: Revista Española de Historia* 43 (1983):281–94.

Chapter Four

1. R. Foulché-Delbosc, "Les oeuvres attribuées a Mendoza," *Revue Hispanique* 32 (1914):1–86. For an additional attribution, see Henry Bonneville, "Sobre el posible autor de *La gata de Juan Crespo*, poem epicoburlesco del Siglo de Oro," in *Actas del Sexto Congreso Internacional de Hispanistas* (Toronto, 1980), 118–22.

2. Edited by R. Foulché-Delbosc, "*Mechánica de Aristóteles*," *Revue Hispanique* 5 (1898):365–405.

3. Edited by Adolfo de Castro, *BAE*, vol. 26: *Curiosidades Bibliográficas* (Madrid, 1855), 1–7.

4. Spivakovsky, 193.

5. Ibid., 282.

6. Charon queries Pier Luigi: "¿No sabes que tu padre se deleita de la nigromancia, y tiene espíritus familiares, trata y habla con ellos; cosa que no solamente la Iglesia, mas el mismo Dios la defiende?" (*BAE*, 36:6).

7. *BAE*, 36:6. Earlier, Charon had predicted to Pier Luigi: "A tu padre le pesa de la grandeza y buena fortuna del Emperador, como aquel que tiene entendido que no ha de consentir que dure tanto tiempo la disolución del clero y la desórden que hay en la Iglesia de Jesucristo, y que ha de salir al cabo con la empresa tan santa que ha tomado de juntar el concilio y remediar, juntamente con las herejías de Alemania, la bellaquería de Roma" (5).

8. *BAE*, 36: 7. Charon had earlier accused Pier Luigi and the pope of

actually forming alliances with the Turks against the emperor: "¿No sabes que el año pasado bajó acá Barbarroja, que la mayor lástima que llevaba era no haberse podido vengar de tu padre de no haber cumplido con el Turco ni con él nada de tanto que les prometió cuando lo de Castro y cuando lo de Tolón? como si tu padre, por mucho que lo intentó pudiese estorbar que los cielos y los hados no favorezcan y prosperen las cosas del Emperador" (2).

9. Edited Adolfo de Castro, *BAE*, vol. 36: *Curiosidades bibliográficas* (Madrid, 1855), 547–50. There also exists a "Respuesta del Capitán Salazar" which some have attributed to Mendoza, although it does not appear to be by him. The reply is readily accessible in Antonio Paz y Melia, *Sales españolas*, in *BAE*, vol. 176 (Madrid, 1964), 37–41.

10. "Si Salazar peleaba tanto, ¿cómo veía tanto? ¿Cómo, estando envuelto con los enemigos, podía ver lo que hacían los amigos? Y si él estaba delante de todos, ¿cómo podía ver lo que hacían los que estaban detrás? y si estaba a mirar y a notar lo que todos hacían, ¿cómo se señalaba primero en todas las ocasiones?" (*BAE*, 36: 547).

11. Ibid., 549: "y no la materna, sino la moderna que se habla en Granada desde el año de 1492 a esta parte."

12. Erika Spivakovsky, "*Lo de La Goleta y Túnez*, A Work of Diego Hurtado de Mendoza," *Hispania* (Madrid) 23 (1963):366–79. The work has been published only once in *Colección de Documentos Inéditos para la Historia de España*, vol. 1 (1842; reprint, Vaduz, 1964), 159–207.

13. *Biblioteca Universalis* (Tiruci, 1545), f. 205ᵛ: "Et nuper ex Arnoldi Arlenii nostri literis cognovi . . . (Didacum Mendociam) Tunetana expeditione historiam latine scripsisse: sui ipse no solum interfecit, sed etiam bona ex parte cum fratribus praefuit."

14. "Sacar la gente del saco fue tan dificultoso, que los días que pasaron de dos que ahí S. M. se detuvo, fue por sacar el campo de la tierra, y no solo los soldados, mas los marineros que poco a poco al olor del saco habían venido, era mayor dificultad sacallos que a la gente de guerra: todos se habían venido, y el armada estaba tan sin quien la marease, que cuasi parecían algunas galeras estar en atarazanal y no surtas a do estaban" (203).

15. Edition consulted: *Lazarillo de Tormes*, ed. Francisco Rico (Barcelona, 1976). For a complete bibliography, see J. V. Ricapito, *Bibliografía razonada y anotada de las obras maestras de la picaresca española* (Madrid, 1980).

16. First proposed in 1605 by José de Sigüenza, *Historia de la Orden de San Jerónimo*, in *Nueva Biblioteca de Autores Españoles*, vol. 12 (Madrid, 1909), 145; this was later supported by Marcel Bataillon, *La vie de Lazarillo de Tormes* (Paris, 1958; translated into Spanish as *Novedad y fecundidad del Lazarillo de Tormes*, Salamanca, 1968).

17. Popularized by Julio Cejador y Frauca, ed., *Lazarillo de Tormes* (Madrid, 1914), and formalized as a serious candidacy by Francisco Márquez Villanueva, "Sebastián de Horozco y el *Lazarillo de Tormes*," *Revista de Filología Española* 41 (1957):253–339.

18. First suggested by A. Morel-Fatio, *Etudes sur l'Espagne*, 1st ser. (Paris, 1888), but given credence by Manuel J. Asensio, "La intención religiosa del *Lazarillo de Tormes* y Juan de Valdés," *Hispanic Review* 27 (1959):72–102.

19. This attribution has been made seriously only by Joseph V. Ricapito, ed., *Lazarillo de Tormes*, 2d ed. (Madrid, 1976).

20. Proposed by A. Rameau, *Le Lazarillo de Tormes, essai d'interpretation, essai d'attribution* (Paris, 1964).

21. Not the dramatist, but a Toledan town crier, supported by Fonger de Haan, *An Outline History of the "Novela Picaresca" in Spain* (New York, 1903), and Fred Abrams, "¿Fue Lope de Rueda el autor del *Lazarillo de Tormes?*" *Hispania* 47 (1964):258–67.

22. Advocated solely by Arturo Marasso, *Estudios de literatura castellana* (Buenos Aires, 1955).

23. See Rico, ed., *Lazarillo*, xv: "El éxito enorme 'desta nonada' inclina a suponer que la composición y desde luego la primera estampa de las fortunas de Lázaro no fueron muy anteriores a 1554"; and Alberto Blecua, ed., *La vida de Lazarillo de Tormes* (Madrid, 1972), 15: "A falta, pues, de un dato firme, lo más plausible—que no siempre se corresponde con la verdad—es fechar el *Lazarillo* en años muy próximos a los de su impresión, quizá inmediatos, lo que explicaría la ausencia general de alusiones a la obra y encajaría mejor en la perspectiva literaria—desarrollo de la autobiografía novelesca y del coloquio erasmista y lucianesco—del medio siglo."

24. Horozco's authorship has its detractors, *videlicet* Ricapito, ed., *Lazarillo*, 40: "A pesar de los muchos paralelos que Márquez encuentre, nosotros mismos vemos una diferencia entre el estilo de Horozco y el del *Lazarillo* que parece ir por otros caminos. Es cierto que el *Refranero* y el *Cancionero* de Horozco comparten muchos elementos, personajes, temas, lugares comunes, etc., pero el espíritu que informa a estas obras es distinto."

25. *Lazarillo*, ed. Rico, 80.

26. See Bataillon, *Novedad*, 24; and Márquez Villanueva, "Sebastián de Horozco," 121 ff. See also J. E. Gillet, "A Note on the *Lazarillo de Tormes*," *Modern Languages Notes* 55 (1940): 130–34, who argues for a date of composition at least after 1547.

27. Alfredo Cavaliere, ed., *La vida de Lazarillo de Tormes* (Naples, 1955).

28. José Caso González, ed., *Lazarillo de Tormes* (Madrid, 1967), and "La primera edición del *Lazarillo de Tormes* y su relación con los textos de 1554," in *Studia Hispanica in Honorem R. Lapesa*, vol. 1 (Madrid, 1972), 189–206.

29. Francisco Rico, "En torno al texto crítico del *Lazarillo de Tormes*," *Hispanic Review* 38 (1970):405–19.

30. Alberto Blecua, ed., *La vida de Lazarillo de Tormes* (Madrid, 1972).

31. "Los tres textos A [Alcalá], B [Burgos], y C [Antwerp] se remontan a un arquetipo común impreso, X, puesto que la puntuación así lo indica; que de este arquetipo deriva, por un lado, B, y por otros un subarquetipo Y del que preceden A y C" (*Lazarillo*, ed. Blecua, 67).

32. "Los textos perdidos X e Y verían la luz muy probablemente en 1553, quizá en 1552, pero no en fecha más temprana" (ibid., 8).

33. A. Rumeau, "Notes aux *Lazarillo*: Les éditions romantiques et Hurtado de Mendoza (1810–1842)," in *Mélanges a la Mémoire de Jean Serrailh*, vol. 2 (Paris, 1966), 301–12.

34. Angel González Palencia, *Del Lazarillo a Quevedo* (Madrid, 1946), 1–40; his edition of *Lazarillo de Tormes* (Zaragoza, 1947); and González Palencia and Mele, 3:206–22.

35. Erika Spivakovsky, "¿Valdés o Mendoza?," *Hispanófila*, no. 12 (1961):15–23: "Todos los atributos concediendo ser Valdés autor potencial de *Lazarillo* (como Asensio los ha compilado perpicaz y sólidamente), pueden extenderse igualmente a Mendoza, pero . . . no todo lo demás que sirve a favor de Don Diego, puede aplicarse a Valdés" (22–23).

36. Erika Spivakovsky, "The *Lazarillo de Tormes* and Mendoza," *Symposium* 15 (1961):271–85.

37. This letter and the arguments based on it have been strongly repudiated by Janie Oliva Scrouch, "El autor del *Lazarillo* sobre una reciente tesis," *Hispanófila*, no. 16 (1963):11–23.

38. Erika Spivakovsky, "New Arguments in Favor of Mendoza's Authorship of the *Lazarillo de Tormes*," *Symposium* 24 (1970):67–80.

39. Claudio Guillén, ed., *Lazarillo de Tormes and El Abencerraje* (New York, 1966), 33.

40. Donald McGrady, "Social Irony in *Lazarillo de Tormes* and Its Implications for Authorship," *Romance Philology* 23 (1969–70):557–67.

41. *Lazarillo*, ed. Rico, 9.

42. Fred Abrams, "Hurtado de Mendoza's Concealed Signatures in the *Lazarillo de Tormes*," *Romance Notes* 15 (1973):341–45.

43. Charles V. Aubrun, "El autor del *Lazarillo*: Un retrato robot," *Cuadernos Hispanoamericanos*, nos. 238–40 (1969):543–55.

44. *Lazarillo*, ed. Rico, 12.

45. Ibid., 80.

Chapter Five

1. According to Nader, *The Mendoza Family*.

2. Spivakovsky, 406. A chronological list of the publications containing Mendoza's letters is on 414–15.

3. Mendoza's Aristotelianism has been closely examined by Erika

Spivakovsky, "Diego Hurtado de Mendoza and Averroism," *Journal of the History of Ideas* 26 (1965):307–26.

4. One example among many is A. A. Parker, "Expansion and Scholarship in Spain," in *The Age of the Renaissance*, ed. Denys Hay (London, 1967), 221–48.

5. The one extensive study on the Spanish verse epistle is Carol L. K. Levine, "The Verse Epistle in Spanish Poetry of the Golden Age" (PhD. diss., Johns Hopkins University, 1974).

Selected Bibliography

PRIMARY SOURCES

Algunas cartas de don Diego Hurtado de Mendoza escritas 1538–1552. Edited by Alberto Vásquez and R. Selden Rose. New Haven: Yale University Press, 1935. A collection of virtually all the extant letters written by Mendoza to Francisco de los Cobos, secretary to the Emperor Charles V, and to Antoine Perrenot de Granvelle, imperial councilor to Charles V and Philip II.

"A tí, Doña Marina": The Poetry of Don Diego Hurtado de Mendoza. Edited by Malcolm C. Batchelor. Havana: Ucar-García, 1959. A study and edition of the autographic manuscript, Esp. 311, in the National Library, Paris. The edition is good, but the introductory material is uncritical and specious.

Carta al Capitán Salazar. Edited by Adolfo de Castro. In *Biblioteca de Autores Españoles*, vol. 36. Madrid: M. Rivadeneyra, 1855, 547–50. The most accessible printed edition of this piece attributed to Mendoza. There are a number of contemporary manuscripts in the Madrid National Library.

Diálogo entre Caronte y el ánima de Pedro Luis Farnesio. Edited by Adolfo de Castro. In *Biblioteca de Autores Españoles*, vol. 36. Madrid: M. Rivadeneyra, 1855, 1–7. The first and most accessible edition of this work attributed to Mendoza, of which a number of manuscripts exist in the Madrid National Library.

Guerra de Granada. Edited by Luis Tribaldos de Toledo. Lisbon: Giraldo de la Viña, 1627. The *princeps* of Mendoza's famous history of the rebellion in Granada.

Guerra de Granada. Edited by Bernardo Blanco de González. Madrid: Castalia, 1970. The latest and most complete edition of Mendoza's history.

Lo de La Goleta y Túnez, año de 1535. Colección de Documentos Inéditos para la Historia de España 1 (1842):159–207. A detailed account of the taking of Tunis from Barbarossa in 1535 (MS Escorial Library). Spivakovsky (*Hispania* [Madrid] 23 [1963]:366–79) supports Mendoza's authorship, asserting it is the Spanish version of Mendoza's "lost" *De Tunetana Expeditione.*

Mechánica de Aristóteles. Edited by R. Foulché-Delbosc. *Revue Hispanique* 5 (1898):365–405. An edition of Mendoza's translation from the Greek.

Obras del insigne caballero don Diego de Mendoza. Edited by Juan Díaz Hidalgo. Madrid: Juan de la Cuesta, 1610. The *princeps* edition of Mendoza's poetry. Republished in its entirety by Adolfo de Castro, *Biblioteca de Autores Españoles*, vol. 32 (Madrid, 1854), 51–103.

Obras poéticas. Edited by William I. Knapp. Madrid: Miguel Ginesta, 1877. The most complete collection of Mendoza's poetic works.

Paraphrasis in Totum Aristotelem. Escorial MS f.II.6. An autograph manuscript of this Latin work is in the Escorial Library.

SECONDARY SOURCES

Abrams, Fred. "Hurtado de Mendoza's Concealed Signatures in the *Lazarillo de Tormes*." *Romance Notes* 15 (1973–74):341–45. The first seven words of *Lazarillo* ("Pues sepa vuestra merced ante todas cosas") contain the words *Urtado, Mendosa, Danteo,* and *Andrea*. Abrams considers such a precise rendition of Mendoza's name and two pseudonyms more than coincidental.

Aubrun, Charles V. "El autor del *Lazarillo*: Un retrato robot." *Cuadernos Hispanoamericanos* 238–40 (1969):543–55. A measured argument for Mendoza's authorship of the *Lazarillo*.

Caro Baroja, Julio. *Ciclos y temas de la historia de España: Los moriscos del Reino de Granada (ensayo de historia social)*. 2d ed. Madrid: ISTMO, 1976. Chapter 6, on the rebellion of Granada, refers extensively to Mendoza's *Guerra de Granada* and offers an analysis of its style and its general attitude towards the events described.

Cossío, José María de. *Fábulas mitológicas en España*. Madrid: Espasa-Calpe, 1952. Contains a close analysis of Mendoza's renditions of Ovid's stories of Iphis and Anaxarete, and Adonis, Hippomenes, and Atalanta (89–97).

Crawford, J. P. W. "Don Diego de Mendoza and Michele Marullo." *Hispanic Review* 6 (1938):346–48. Two of Mendoza's classical sonnets—"De Saladino" and "¿Qué cuerpo yace en esta sepultura?"—are from Michele Marullus, *Hymni et Epigrammata* (Florence, 1497).

————"Notes on the Poetry of Diego Hurtado de Mendoza." *Modern Language Review* 23 (1928):346–51. Attempts to establish a relationship between the "Marina" and "Marfira" in Mendoza's poetry and doña Marina de Aragón (1523–49). Also notes sources for the two sonnets "El hombre que doliente está a muerte" (Ausias March) and "En cierto hospedaje do posaba" (Alciati's *Emblemata*).

Darieaux, M. "Diego Hurtado de Mendoza et le *Lazarillo de Tormes*." *Hispania* (Paris) 3 (1920):17–25.

Darst, David H. *Juan Boscán*. Boston: Twayne, 1978. Examines Mendoza's verse epistle "A Boscán" in the context of the Catalan's reply ("Epístola a don Diego de Mendoza").

_____ "El pensamiento histórico del granadino Diego Hurtado de Mendoza." *Hispania: Revista Española de Historia* 43 (1983): 281–94. A study of Mendoza's prose writings, with emphasis on *Guerra de Granada*.

Fesenmair, Joh. *Don Diego Hurtado de Mendoza: Ein spanischer Humanist des XVI Jahrhunderst*. Munich: H. Kutzner, 1882.

Foulché-Delbosc, R. "Etude sur la *Guerra de Granada* de don Diego Hurtado de Mendoza." *Revue Hispanique* 1 (1894):101–61. A solid study of Mendoza's book. Includes a biography of the years 1569–75, a bibliography of all editions, a resumé of the 1627 text, and a bibliography of the many manuscripts.

_____ "Les oeuvres attribuées a Mendoza." *Revue Hispanique* 32 (1914): 1–86. Examines twenty-one prose works attributed over the years to Mendoza. Also publishes for the first time a group of poems that bear his name from various manuscripts.

_____ "Un point contesté de la vie de don Diego Hurtado de Mendoza." *Revue Hispanique* 2 (1895):208–303. Studies the relationship between Mendoza and Philip II, especially as concerns don Diego's quarrel in the royal palace with Diego de Leyva on July 23, 1568. Also presents various documents concerning King Philip's acceptance of Mendoza's books and classical artifacts.

González Ollé, Fernando. "Interpretación del 'perqué' de don Diego de Mendoza." *Revista de Filología Española* 47 (1964):449–51. An interpretation of two lines of a Mendoza poem that begins the *Cancionero de Palacio*: "Por qué andan a muriellos / los que viven en baxuras" means "¿Por qué se ocupan de (*o* andan tras) los ratoncillos / los que viven en medio de (*o* entre) basuras?"

González Palencia, Angel, and Mele, Eugenio. *Vida y obras de don Diego Hurtado de Mendoza*. 3 vols. Madrid: Instituto de Valencia de don Juan Primero, 1941–43. Fully documented, this is the best and most complete biography of Hurtado de Mendoza in Spanish. Volumes 1–2 concern the life of don Diego; volume 3 discusses his literary works and includes important documents in one hundred and nineteen appendices.

Keniston, Hayward. *Francisco de los Cobos: Secretary to the Emperor Carlos V*. Pittsburgh: University of Pittsburgh Press, 1959. Competent survey of the life and times of the man with whom Mendoza carried on most of his correspondence while in Venice.

Nader, Helen. "Josephus and Diego Hurtado de Mendoza." *Romance Philology* 26 (1972):554–55. Attempts unsuccessfully to prove that when composing *Guerra de Granada* Mendoza used Josephus's *De Bello Judaico* as his historiographical model.

_____ *The Mendoza Family in the Spanish Renaissance 1350 to 1550*. New Brunswick: Rutgers University Press, 1979. Penetrating survey of the Mendoza family's influence and control of Hispanic letters in the fifteenth century. The last chapter, "The Failure of the Caballero Renaissance," discusses don Diego's place in the Mendoza humanist tradition.

Reichenberger, Arnold G. "Boscán's *Epístola a Mendoza.*" *Hispanic Review* 17 (1949):1–17. The study concludes with a sensitive comparison of Mendoza's *Aurea mediocritas* and Boscán's Neo-Platonism.

Rivers, Elias L. "The Horatian Epistle and Its Introduction into Spanish Literature." *Hispanic Review* 22 (1954):175–94. Compares and contrasts the meter, style, tone, intent, and subject matter of Garcilaso's epistle to Boscán, Mendoza's to Boscán, and Boscán's to Mendoza.

Rodríguez Villa, Antonio. *Noticia biográfica y documentos históricos relativos a don Diego Hurtado de Mendoza.* Madrid: Aribau, 1883.

Rothberg, Irving, P. "Hurtado de Mendoza and the Green Epigrams." *Hispanic Review* 26 (1958):171–87. Examines Mendoza's many debts to the Greek Anthology.

Rumeau, A. "Notes aux *Lazarillo.* Les éditions romantiques et Hurtado de Mendoza (1810–1842)." In *Mélanges a la Mémoire de Jean Serrailh,* vol. 2. Paris: Institut d'Etudes Hispaniques, 1966, 301–12. Shows that all of the editions of *Lazarillo* from 1810 to 1842 were attributed to Mendoza only because they all were following a statement to that effect by Bouterwek in 1804, which was incorporated in the Paris 1813 edition.

Scrouch, Janie Oliva. "El autor del *Lazarillo* sobre una reciente tesis." *Hispanófila*, no. 19 (1963):11–23. A sharp attack on Spivakovsky's methodology for "proving" Mendoza's authorship of the *Lazarillo.* While Scrouch does not deny don Diego's paternity, she does reject all previous arguments in his favor.

Señán y Alonso. Eloy. *Don Diego Hurtado de Mendoza: Apuntes biográficocríticos.* Jeréz: El Guadalete, 1886.

Simón Díaz, José. "Hurtado de Mendoza (Diego)." In *Bibliografía de la literatura hispánica,* vol. 11. Madrid: CSIC, 1976, 681–97. A complete and well-documented bibliography (nos. 5628–83) of Mendoza's works as well as a partial list of studies on his writings.

Spivakovsky, Erika. "Diego Hurtado de Mendoza and Averroism." *Journal of the History of Ideas* 26 (1965):307–26. Mendoza was a philosophical "nonconformist" for his age, as his preference for Averroism rather than Thomism demonstrates. He "carried in his mind a unique amalgamation of the newest Italian philosophies plus the Spanish-Arabic heritage," "a unique blend of Christian, Arabic, and classical heritage."

————"The *Lazarillo de Tormes* and Mendoza." *Symposium* 15 (1961):271–85. Sees the *Lazarillo* as a parody of Mendoza's own experiences. Many people in the work are also caricatures: blind man—Paul III, young squire—Charles V.

————"Lo de La Goleta y Túnez, A Work of Diego Hurtado de Mendoza." *Hispania* (Madrid) 23 (1963):366–79. Makes a strong case for attributing this work to Mendoza.

———— "Mendoza's Renunciation of Fame as Revealed in his *Carta* VI from Alcántara." *Hispania* 53 (1970):220–24. Towards the end of 1553, Mendoza decided to refrain from seeking literary fame and consequently not to publish any of his prose or poetry. Spivakovsky claims that this decision and the reasons for it are poetized in the poem "Cuando al hombre sin abrigo."

———— "New Arguments in Favor of Mendoza's Authorship of the *Lazarillo de Tormes*." *Symposium* 24 (1970):67–80. Suggests the *Lazarillo* is a parody of don Fernando Alvarez de Toledo, Duke of Alba (1507–82). He and Mendoza were friends when young, although in 1549 the friendship terminated because of differences of opinion concerning the political situation in Italy.

———— "Some notes on the Relations between don Diego Hurtado de Mendoza and don Alonso de Granada Venegas." *Archivum* 14 (1964):221–32. Documents the close friendship between Mendoza and his distant relative the *morisco granadino* don Alonso de Granada Venegas y Rengifo.

————*Son of the Alhambra: Don Diego Hurtado de Mendoza*, 1504–1575. Austin: University of Texas Press, 1970. A well-written account of don Diego's life and times. The book makes available to the English-speaking world the vast wealth of information compiled by González Palencia and Mele, and presents it in a lively, readable style and tempo. The Italian sojourn (1539–52) is especially well recounted.

———— "¿Valdés o Mendoza?" *Hispanófila*, no. 12 (1961):15–23. Argues against Asensio's attribution of the *Lazarillo* to Juan Valdés. Shows that the same arguments to prove Valdés's authorship work as well for don Diego's.

———— "Which don Alonso Venegas? Two Episodes from the *Guerra de Granada* and the *Historia del rebelión*." *Renaissance News* 17 (1964):193–96. The man offered the kingship of Almería by the rebellious Moriscos and referred to by Mendoza as Alonso Venegas is actually Alonso de Granada Venegas, a close friend of the poet.

Torre y Franco-Romero, Lucas de. "Don Diego Hurtado de Mendoza no fue el autor de la *Guerra de Granada*." *Boletín de la Real Academia de la Historia* 64 (1914):461–501, 557–96; 65 (1914):28–47, 273–302, 369–415. This lengthy study attempts to prove that the *Guerra de Granada* was written by Juan Rufo, author of the epic poem *La Austriada* (1584). Torre's thesis has never been taken seriously.

Triwedi, Mitchell D. "On Mendoza's Sonnet to His Book." *Romance Notes* 12 (1970–71):413–15. An analysis of the poem "Libro, pues vas ante quien puede."

Index